# A POCKET GUIDE TO
# CARS

# A POCKET GUIDE TO
# CARS

Andrew Montgomery

This is a Parragon Publishing Book
First published in 2006

Parragon Publishing
Queen Street House
4 Queen Street
Bath, BA1 1HE, UK

Produced by Atlantic Publishing

See page 256 for photographs copyright details
Text © Parragon Books Ltd 2006

ISBN   1-40547-338-X

Printed in China

# CONTENTS

# INTRODUCTION

E ver since the automobile was first invented at the end of the 19th century, man has been competing to build ever faster and more exciting models. It wasn't enough just to get from A to B – it had to be in the quickest time or offer the most exciting driving experience. Over the years technological advances have led to increasing power, which coupled with the science of aerodynamics has led to ever more performance being wrung out of the automobile engine, even in everyday cars.

In the early days, before the First World War, cars in Europe were sumptuous carriages for the wealthy few, while in the United States, Henry Ford endeavored to set the country people free – via the Model T – and thus helped, significantly, to enable the social and economic mobility that has, assisted by the collapse of the old empires, made America the most powerful and dynamic nation on earth.

The "Roaring Twenties" saw the creation of fabulous luxury cars intended to appeal to the vanity of bright young things and shady characters alike, but Hispano-Suiza, Isotta-Fraschini, Bentley, Bugatti, Marmon, Duesenberg, Auburn and Cord were all destroyed by the Wall Street crash.

The Second World War brought huge advances in design and the use of new materials. After the war, America once more raced ahead whilst shattered European economies – not to mention Japan's – struggled to get back on their feet. By the 1960s, however, they had not merely caught up but were threatening the home markets of the "Big Three" American manufacturers. Since then, merger, takeover, collaboration and, all too often, collapse has been the lot of car companies as they struggle to compete in a fickle and unstable market. Where once, not so long ago, it seemed impossible for manufacturers to turn out sufficient cars to meet the public's demand, now massive over-production has led to acres of unsold vehicles and near suicidal discounting. Many manufacturers have perished: Wolseley, Riley, Austin, Morris, Standard, Vanguard,

Hillman, Sunbeam, Jensen, Jowett – and those are just a selection of British makes that have disappeared since the end of the Second World War. The oldest manufacturer in the United States, Oldsmobile, has gone now too, and with it the heritage of the "Curved Dash Olds" – the first volume production car in the world. In truth, only a handful of independent motor manufacturers now exist. Almost all of the grand marques are now the vassals of great, global corporations: Ford, General Motors, Daimler-Chrysler, Citroën/ Peugeot, Volkswagen and Fiat. Rolls-Royce and Bentley are both owned by German companies while Mercedes and BMW SUVs are built in America.

This celebration of the most exciting performance cars of the post-war era covers more than 130 different models, selected across the years right up to the present day. All the major icons are here, as well as a few unusual and exciting models. Each is special – beautifully engineered, with explosive performance and designed for the true driving experience. Every model is covered in loving detail, with a glorious color photograph, an easy-reference fact box and entertaining text giving the key information. Cars are arranged alphabetically so it is easy to find a particular model, but the year of manufacture is also highlighted so that they can be placed in context.

We love cars for all kinds of reasons. They symbolize who we are, or who we think we are, or who we'd like to be.

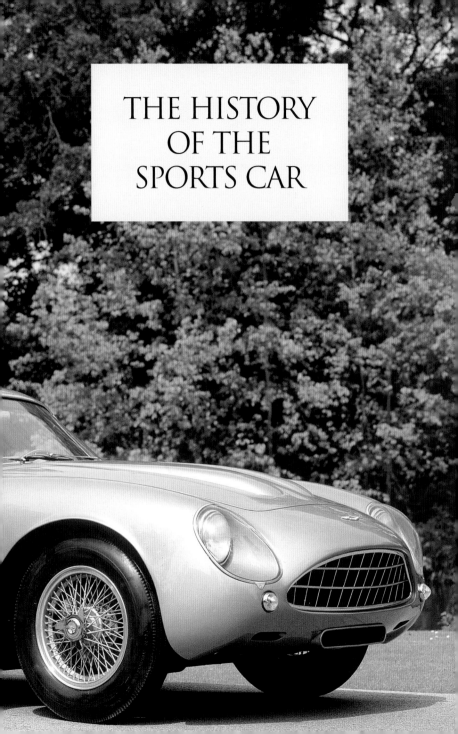

# THE HISTORY
# OF THE
# SPORTS CAR

**H**ow did the sports car come about? I guess the same way that the race horse came about. At first, the horse was employed simply as a means of transport or as a beast of burden, but soon some people started to derive pleasure from the sensation of being able to harness and control power far greater than their own and to cover ground more swiftly than others. It can't have been too long before selective breeding was employed to increase speed and improve agility, thus the cart horse sired the Derby winner while the Model T begat the Mustang – and let's face it: horse power is still what it's all about.

We're dealing here with the triumph of performance over practicality. There's no need for cars to go faster. In nearly all countries today there are blanket speed limits, and in many countries – the United States for one – the sheer volume of traffic on the roads makes the attainment of the speed limit, never mind the breaking of it, all but impossible most of the time. Even so, there can be very, very few private cars, or even commercial vehicles, come to that, and certainly no sports cars that are not capable of speeds in excess of that allowed by statute. Why should this be? Why should this be allowed? Why are motor manufacturers permitted to produce and purvey machines that are patently obviously designed to break the law? We have become deeply attached to the prospect of power and performance – of potency – that the sports car promises us. Speed is a drug. It's a stimulant, an intoxicant and an aphrodisiac. James Bond drank vodka martinis, had his cigarettes hand-made and drove an Aston Martin DB5. All of those had the potential to damage his health (and wealth), seriously – but look what they did for his image.

Until 1895, British law stated that a motor vehicle traveling on the Queen's Highway had to be preceded by a person bearing a red banner to warn of its approach. The speed limit was raised to 20 mph in 1903 and remained there until 1930 – by which time Sir Henry Segrave had set a world land speed record of well over 200 mph at Daytona Beach. Segrave was also the first Englishman (actually, he was half American and had spent his boyhood in Ireland) to win a Grand Prix, at Tours in 1923 driving a 2-liter Sunbeam at an average speed of 75.3 mph.

In the very early days of motor sport, continental Europeans, notably the French, had things pretty much their own way. The first formally organized automobile

*Above: The 1954 Mercedes 300SL, known as the Gullwing Mercedes, was one of the fastest cars on the road in its day with a top speed of 154 mph.*

competition over the approximately 80 miles between Paris and Rouen was run in 1894 and sponsored (like cycling's epic Tour de France, which was first contested nearly a decade later) by a newspaper – *Le Petit Journal*. A steam traction engine came in first but was disqualified on a technicality and so the prize of 5,000 francs went to a Peugeot, which had covered the course at an average speed of less than 12 mph – even so, the stage was set.

The first true sports car arrived in 1901 in the elegant shape of the innovative Mercedes, which was intended specifically for fast, rather than comfortable, travel. It was a car for driving rather than for being driven in. Designed by Wilhelm Maybach of the Daimler company, the Mercedes was named after the 10-year-old daughter of valued customer and associate Emil Jellinek. It featured a low-slung pressed steel chassis, a fan-cooled honeycomb radiator, mechanical inlet valves – replacing the "atmospheric" type that were most common then – and a proper throttle. The Mercedes was capable of 60 mph – the magical, almost unimaginable, mile-a-minute.

At first, most sporting cars were powered by simple, side-valve engines. The 1911 Alfonso Hispano-Suiza, designed by Marc Birkigt, used a 3.6-liter four-cylinder engine and achieved a respectable 70–75 mph. The 1912 "Prince Henry" Vauxhall, designed by Laurence Pomeroy, was powered by a potentially high-revving, 3-liter side-valve engine. The highly efficient, twin overhead-camshaft engine design, still employed by most sports cars today, was first introduced by Peugeot in 1912.

The 1913 Vauxhall, with its 4.5-liter, "30/98" power plant, was able to reach over 80 mph on the road and when tuned for the racetrack could achieve an incredible 100 mph. It set the standard for British sports cars of the twenties. During this period the newly created masterpiece of W.O. Bentley, built in the London suburb of Cricklewood, along with Sunbeam of Wolverhampton, became Vauxhall's great rival. Bentley's first car, the 3 liter, launched in 1921, could hit 90 mph in road tune. It was powered by an overhead-camshaft engine, a configuration that had been a significant feature of aero

*Below: The 1952 Bentley R Type Continental, the prototype of which completed five laps of the Le Mans circuit at an average speed of just under 120 mph.*

*Above: The Fiat 8V was the company's first post-war sports car. It was primarily intended as a competition model and fewer than 120 cars were made before production stopped in 1954.*

engine design since the First World War. Bentley went on to produce an 8-liter model that could top the elusive 100 mph. Thanks largely to financial support from the massively wealthy and eccentric Woolf Barnato, Bentley briefly dominated sports car racing, winning the Le Mans 24-hour race on five occasions between 1924 and 1930.

Grand Prix events, by contrast, were the preserve of continental Europeans. Fiat and Alfa Romeo from Italy, Bugatti from France and Mercedes-Benz from Germany were the main competitors for Grand Prix laurels. Just as today, racing improved the breed, and technological advances developed for competition trickled down, eventually to be incorporated into the designs of everyday motor cars. The most significant mechanical innovation of this period was the supercharger – basically an engine-driven pump that forces air into the cylinders to give more effective combustion. First introduced in 1923 on the Fiat 805, the "blower" was an essential part of racing cars until the fifties. Superchargers soon arrived on road cars as well. In 1931 the fabulous, supercharged Alfa Romeo 8C, designed by Vittorio Jano, could reach 115 mph on the road. The Type 55 Bugatti could reach 110 mph and was only one stage of tune removed from a Grand Prix racer. In Germany, the SSK from Mercedes-Benz was powered by a massive 7.1-liter supercharged engine and could easily top 110 mph.

In 1929 a newcomer to the market, Bayerische
Motoren Werke – or Bavarian Motor Works – began
producing cars under the BMW marque. They had
previously built aero engines (hence their propeller
badge) and motorcycles, and this experience proved
invaluable as they began to develop performance cars.
BMW's products became increasingly sophisticated –
when the 328 sports car was launched, in 1936, it
immediately made most other sports cars of the time
appear obsolete.

The two-seater 328 had aerodynamic bodywork
with integral headlights, a 2-liter cross-pushrod valve
engine, rack and pinion steering and hydraulic brakes.
It was lightweight, nimble, and could reach 95 mph on
the road, with competition-tuned versions topping
110 mph on the track. By contrast, the 2-liter Aston
Martin, although exquisitely built and exclusive, was
also very expensive and had a design, both bodily and
mechanically, that dated back to the twenties. Its much
heavier construction limited top speed to a shade over
80 mph.

In America, Ransom Eli Olds had been the first
volume motor manufacturer in the United States with
his horseless buggy, the Curved-Dash Oldsmobile.
Henry Ford had started out wanting to build racing
cars but he'd ended up gaining immortality by
pioneering mass-produced motoring for the masses
with his magnificent "Tin Lizzy" – the Model T. By the
1920s, America was producing cars whose design and
performance was more than a match for even the most

*Right: Like Ford's Model T, the Ford Mustang was built with an eye
to economy. The original Mustang was produced almost entirely
from stock parts.*

sophisticated European machinery. While Bentley was still relying on massive, long-stroke, "blown" four-cylinder engines in what Ettore Bugatti aptly described as "the fastest trucks in the world," Cadillac was busily building not one but two V16s and Marmon was making a third. The Stutz Bearcat dominated oval track racing and the J Series Duesenbergs provided a level of prestige and performance that eclipsed, briefly, even the offerings of Rolls-Royce, Isotta-Fraschini and Bugatti. The Great Depression that followed the Wall Street crash of October 1929 drove the makers of many of America's most beautiful and exciting cars to … the wall. Cadillac survived (as "The Standard of the World") only because in was part of the then seemingly indestructible General Motors Corporation.

Many noble British and Continental marques either disappeared or were reduced to mere ciphers during the dark days of the Depression, but in the 1930s a little ray of sunshine did appear in the form of the attractive and affordable MG. The MG (Morris Garages) marque was created by Cecil Kimber, a stylist of formidable talent. His boat-tailed, Morris-Minor-based M-type Midget was powered by a lowly 847 cc single-overhead-camshaft engine and was only capable of 65 mph – but it cost an affordable £175. His J2 of 1932 set the styling parameters for traditional sports cars for the next thirty years. A revised version of the Midget, the J2 had humped scuttles, cutaway doors,

*Below: In the 1960s the MG B became the world's most popular sports car.*

a bolster fuel tank and flowing wings. It not only delighted European enthusiasts, but also captured the hearts of American servicemen stationed in England during the Second World War.

After the Second World War, most fast car manufacturers could only offer warmed-over, pre-war models, but even these were eagerly snapped up by a car-hungry public. Britain remained faithful to its traditional, open two-seaters, which had also now found a ready market in America, but continental Europe recognized that closed bodywork was more aerodynamically efficient. Many continental sports cars therefore featured coupé coachwork. The Continent was also home to two new marques – Porsche and Ferrari – which between them created some of the greatest performance cars of the post-war years. Enzo Ferrari began production of his 166 model in 1948, and in the same year Ferry Porsche, son of Ferdinand, himself the father of the Volkswagen, built the legendary 356.

With the American economy booming in the 1950s, her closest ally, Great Britain, became the largest provider of fast cars for her vast market. Jaguar and MG roadsters were joined by the new Austin-Healey and the revived Triumph marque. Most Aston Martins and Bentleys headed west too, doing their bit for the export drive.

In 1953, with the dawning of the New Elizabethan Age in Britain, America got her very own, post-war sports car – the Chevrolet Corvette. Designed by the legendary stylist Harley Earl and engineered by the equally renowned Ed Cole, the Corvette featured a road-hugging profile and fiberglass bodywork. In many ways the car was an anachronism. A giant company churning out 1.3 million family cars a year had no business making a tiny quantity of hand-made sports cars, using special materials, but Harley Earl was a true car enthusiast and produced a sports car, based on stock mechanicals, that would become internationally acclaimed. The first model fell far short of what he was trying to achieve, but luckily it caught the attention of the American car-buying public and survived to go on to much bigger and better things. Ford was not to be left behind either – in 1955 it launched the sporty two-seater Thunderbird as an indirect competitor to the Corvette, featuring a "proper" V8 engine as opposed to the original Corvette's ancient "Stovebolt Six." The T-bird may have seemed big and sloppy for a sports car by European standards, but Stateside it was the real deal, with gorgeous styling and a name to die for – and it was all-American too.

In the 1960s, sales of fast cars boomed as the first post-war generation reached car-buying age. Britain continued to stick with the open two-seater and Europe with the coupé, but America was continuing to harness the awesome and growing power of the

mighty V8 engine, giving birth to incredibly successful models such as the Ford Mustang. However, the boom came to an abrupt halt in the early seventies, with the outbreak of the Arab-Israeli War in 1973. Overnight, oil prices went through the roof and the subsequent, massive rise in the price of gasoline, coupled with a 55 mph speed limit and the threat of fuel rationing, made many people think twice before buying a 7-liter gas-guzzler. The downturn affected Britain more than most and sounded the death knell for many sports cars. Despite continually rising fuel prices the turbocharger arrived and the "blower" made a comeback in the 1980s, having languished in the doldrums for fifty years. Once used only in race cars, it now appeared in the higher spec models from mainstream competitors such as Mercedes, Ford and Volkswagen.

So where do we go in the future, and in what? Will the current fashion for retro styling continue – cars that look like the ones that were cool when the designers themselves were kids – or will the challenges of pollution and depleted oil reserves bring some amazing transformation? Will looking back over the fantastic creations that fill these pages give us an insight into what sports cars will look like in the future? Perhaps. In the early 1920s the indomitable Alfred P. Sloan circulated a memorandum to senior staff at General Motors to the effect that the basic design of the automobile – in engineering terms – had been established and was unlikely to change radically. He was right – in many ways it hasn't. However fast a car can go potentially, there are speed limits and safety restraints holding it back. The best way to keep the car-buying public buying cars is to make them look different. New technologies will surely give us cleaner and more efficient power plants and a more environmentally aware generation will be starting to favor low-emission – or even no-emission – fuels. Whatever happens, the sports car will remain a personal choice item and the lure of speed will always remain with us.

*Left: Chevrolet's Corvette Sting Ray, a classic American sports car introduced in 1963.*

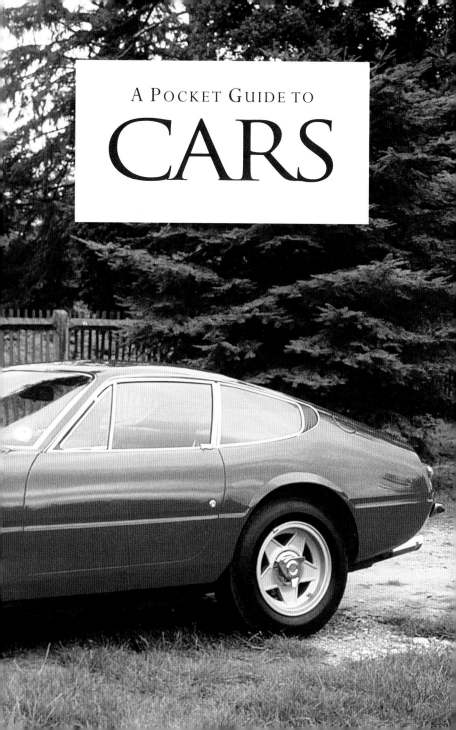

A POCKET GUIDE TO

# CARS

# AC ACE 1953

AC Cars took its title from its first product, the three-wheeled AutoCarrier of 1908. By the fifties, however, things had got a little more exciting in the leafy, riverside village of Thames Ditton, Surrey, England. The AC Ace was inspired by John Tojeiro's magnificent, Bristol-engined racing cars. Built around a space frame with styling that echoed the Ferrari 166 Barchetta, the car's performance was as uncompromising as its looks. A range of BMW-derived Bristol engines were offered as alternatives to AC's venerable, 2-liter six-cylinder power plant, all with four-speed transmission. A closed coupé version (the Aceca) was introduced in 1955 and the more civilized – though not quite civilized enough – Greyhound, built on a slightly longer wheelbase, with sophisticated, independent front suspension, came along in 1960. Bristol's move to American V8 power initially threatened the Ace with extinction but it was American V8 power that would ultimately render it immortal – as the Cobra.

| ENGINE: | (Bristol 100D) Front-mounted, six cylinder, in line | OUTPUT: | 120 bhp @ 6000 rpm |
|---|---|---|---|
| | | TOP SPEED: | 115 mph |
| CAPACITY: | 1971 cc | ACCELERATION: | 0–60 in 9.2 seconds |

# AC COBRA 1962

Unquestionably one of the most iconic, truly "legendary" motor cars ever constructed, the AC Cobra was bred out of English tradition and American innovation. Carroll Shelby had enjoyed a spectacular career as a driver, winning at Le Mans with Ray Salvadori in an Aston Martin DBR1 in 1959. The following year, however, he was diagnosed with a heart condition and decided to concentrate on building a car that would end Ferrari's dominance on the track. By shoe-horning a 289 cid (4.7 liters) Ford V8 (later to become a 427 cid/6.9 liters) into an AC Ace chassis, beefing up the suspension and fitting massive rims, Shelby – in collaboration with AC's Charles Hurlock – produced a masterpiece, capable of speeds well in excess of 160 mph. Amazingly, these monsters were regularly tested on public roads by locally based racing drivers such as John Hodges. Shelby's dream came true in 1964 when the Cobra finally defeated the almost-mythical Ferrari GTO at Le Mans.

| | | | |
|---|---|---|---|
| **ENGINE:** | Front-mounted, V8 | **TOP SPEED:** | 138 mph |
| **CAPACITY:** | 4727 cc (289 cid) | **ACCELERATION:** | 0–60 in 5.6 seconds |
| **OUTPUT:** | 300 bhp @ 5700 rpm | | |

# ALFA ROMEO MONTREAL 1970

To celebrate the World's Fair – Expo '67 – in Montreal, Alfa Romeo produced an elegant "concept car" styled by Bertone. Like most styling exercises, it was much admired, but nobody seriously expected it to be offered to the public. In 1970, however, it was – powered by a lightweight, 2.6-liter V8 engine that was nothing less than a detuned version of that used by Carlo Chiti in Alfa's Type 33 sports racing car. Despite its racing pedigree, fuel-injection rendered the car remarkably tractable in traffic and its running gear – though it came from Alfa's stock sedan range, along with a fabulous five-speed transmission – provided an excellent ride and handling at speed. No attempt was made to pretend that the Montreal was anything but a two-seater and it remains a largely undiscovered gem – a true Grand Tourer in the classic mold with delightful period styling touches, the slatted vents in the roof pillars being echoed in the retractable headlight covers.

| | |
|---|---|
| **Engine:** | Front-mounted, V8 |
| **Capacity:** | 2593 cc |
| **Output:** | 200 @ 6500 rpm |
| **Top Speed:** | 140 mph |
| **Acceleration:** | 0–60 in 7.1 seconds |

# ALFA ROMEO SZ 1989

Alfa Romeo's distinguished history
stretches back to before the First
World War. The company's enviable
reputation is built on a combination
of performance and style and both
these qualities are well demonstrated,
in fact defined, by the SZ. Powered by
Alfa's gorgeous all-alloy V6 engine,
bored out to 3 liters, with their
signature trans-axle transmission
layout and running gear derived from
competition versions of the 75
saloon, this limited-production model
(1000 coupés, 800 convertibles)
delivers everything that a driver could
desire – and more. Power delivery is
smooth and progressive and
seemingly endless and, with near
perfect weight distribution, road
holding is genuinely awesome.
Clothed in alarmingly angular
bodywork, styled by Zagato, the SZ is
capable of turning heads without
turning a wheel. A glorious
juxtaposition of apparent
contradictions, the car is as brutal to
look at as it is beautiful to drive: a
true classic from a long line of classic
sports cars.

| | |
|---|---|
| **ENGINE:** | Front-mounted, V6 |
| **CAPACITY:** | 2,959 cc |
| **OUTPUT:** | 210 @ 6200 rpm |
| **TOP SPEED:** | 155 mph |
| **ACCELERATION:** | 0–60 in 6.8 seconds |

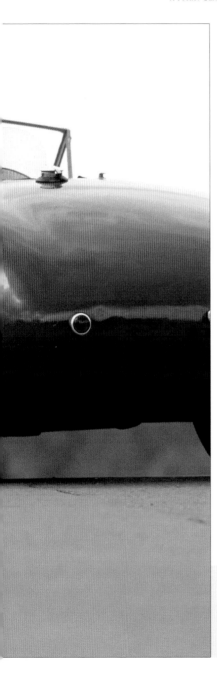

# ALLARD J2 1949

Sidney Allard's company, based in
Clapham in south London, had built
racing specials between the wars and
offered a very basic – crude, in fact –
open sports car (the K1) in 1946. This
was followed by a succession of
variants, which gradually gained in
refinement, culminating in the P1
saloon in which Allard won the 1952
Monte Carlo Rally. The J2, however,
represented what might well be
termed Allard's basic principles.
Bodywork was pared back to a bare
minimum – cycle wings, removable
doors, optional aero screens and so
on, while the maximum possible
performance was supplied via the
fitting of American V8 engines of
ever-increasing capacity and power.
The most renowned of the line were
the Cadillac-powered versions of the
early fifties. Fitted with three-speed
transmission, they could achieve over
80 mph in bottom gear and leave cars
like the Jaguar XK120 standing.
Fewer than 200 examples were built
– the survivors being hugely valued
by collectors – and by 1964
production had ceased, but a 50th
anniversary model has been
announced and orders are being
taken.

| | |
|---|---|
| **ENGINE:** | Front-mounted, V8 |
| **CAPACITY**: | 331 cid |
| **OUTPUT:** | 160 bhp @ 4000 rpm |
| **TOP SPEED:** | 130 mph |
| **ACCELERATION:** | 0–60 in 7.0 seconds |

# ALVIS TE21 1966

The archetypal Gentleman's Motor, the handsome Alvis rose from humble beginnings in the shape of the 1920 10/30. Before long the company was producing cars that delivered real performance with total reliability and introducing such innovations as front-wheel drive. The company's Silver Eagle and Crested Eagle, produced in the 1930s, were stylish and sophisticated – and fast, despite their "solid" construction. During the Second World War, Alvis produced a range of military vehicles – a line that would one day eclipse its civilian cars. The 1950s saw a succession of refined roadsters and sports saloons – notably the TB and "Grey Lady" models – that continued to prize comfort and build quality over flashy styling. This philosophy continued into the 1960s with the TD21, the TE21 and the TF21 – the last being built effectively under British Leyland supervision as the company was bought out by Rover in 1965. The splendid, stately-yet-sporting bodywork, available in fixed and drop head coupé form, was inspired by the Swiss coachbuilders Graber and was perfectly complemented by the beautifully refined, silk-smooth six-cylinder triple-carburetor power plant.

| ENGINE: | Front-mounted, six cylinder, in line | OUTPUT: | 150 bhp @ 4750 rpm |
| CAPACITY: | 2993 cc | TOP SPEED: | 120 mph |
| | | ACCELERATION: | 0–60 in 8.0 seconds |

# ASTON MARTIN DB4 (ZAGATO) 1961

Styled by Carrozzeria Touring of Milan, the DB4's curvaceous body was *superleggera* – super light – being formed of aluminum panels over a tubular steel structure and built under license at Aston Martin's own factory at Newport Pagnell in Buckinghamshire, England. Power was supplied by an all-new, all-alloy, six-cylinder twin-cam engine. The DB4's debut at the Paris Motor Show was a sensation and it became the best-selling model in the company's history. A more powerful Vantage version followed, along with an elegant Volante convertible, but the DB4's ultimate incarnation was the brutal, Zagato-styled GT of 1961. Only 19 of these special short-wheelbase versions were produced, capable of accelerating to 60 mph in six seconds and topping 160 mph – sensational performance for the time and still impressive today. The DB4 was replaced by the DB5 in 1964. The DB5 had all the advantages of its predecessor plus the kudos of being James Bond's favored mode of transport. The DB6 of 1966 gained size and weight and a Kamm tail, while abandoning the construction techniques of its illustrious forebears.

| | | | |
|---|---|---|---|
| **ENGINE:** | Front-mounted, six cylinder, in line | **OUTPUT:** | 240 bhp @ 5500 rpm |
| | | **TOP SPEED:** | 140 mph |
| **CAPACITY:** | 3670 cc | **ACCELERATION:** ' | 0–60 in 9.3 seconds |

# ASTON MARTIN DB9 VOLANTE 2006

The Aston Martin DB9 was conceived at the outset as both a coupé and a convertible: the Volante. The styling of this elegant new addition to the range used computer modeling so that invisible "hard-pressure" zones could be included to cope with low-speed impacts – the "bumpers" are invisible and the number plate is part of the crash structure. In the event of a rollover, pop-up hoops appear from behind the rear head rests. The unique "swan-wing" doors rise at a 12-degree angle to enable ease of access. The interior is luxuriously comfortable, hand-trimmed in wood and leather and with a full range of technological aids to please even the most gadget-loving driver – although the display is not distracting, as even the satellite navigation screen moves silently away when not in use. It takes one push of a button and a mere seventeen seconds to raise or lower the roof. The driver sits low to achieve "a rich driving experience." At the heart of the DB9 is the all-aluminum, 6-liter V12 engine, which gives an impressive top speed of 186 mph. It is mounted as far back as possible to give the car its superb balance.

| | |
|---|---|
| **Engine:** | Mid front-mounted, V12 |
| **Capacity:** | 5935 cc |
| **Output:** | 450 bhp @ 6000 rpm |
| **Top Speed:** | 186 mph |
| **Acceleration:** | 0–60 in 4.9 seconds |

# ASTON MARTIN VANQUISH 2001

When Aston Martin passed into Ford's ownership in 1987, the necessary funding to restore it to its rightful position as a world-class performance car became available, as did the will to achieve this goal in the shape of Ford's President, Jac Nasser – himself the owner of a DB4! At a time of general motor industry malaise, if not crisis, Nasser had the courage and the foresight to back the Vanquish project. Ford's Cosworth racing division were instrumental in producing the V12 engine, by mating two Montego V6s on to a common crankshaft. Though the styling recalls the DBs of the fifties and sixties, the materials used in the car's construction are all state-of-the-art. The transmission tunnel is made from carbon fiber and the body panels of extruded aluminum. The massive output of the Vanquish's V12 is transmitted via a six-speed gearbox, which may be used manually, via race-car-style paddles, or in fully automatic mode. Despite the Aston's traditional front-engine-rear-drive layout, road holding is remarkable and the car is once more a viable challenge to Italy and Germany's finest.

| | |
|---|---|
| **ENGINE:** | Front-mounted, V12 |
| **CAPACITY:** | 5925 cc |
| **OUTPUT:** | 460 bhp @ 6500 rpm |
| **TOP SPEED:** | 196 mph |
| **ACCELERATION:** | 0–60 in 4.8 seconds |

# ASTON MARTIN V8 VANTAGE 2006

The future prosperity of Aston Martin is pinned on the elegant new V8 Vantage, which is priced to bring Aston Martin ownership to a whole new range of hotshot customers who would otherwise be aspiring to a Porsche 911. Like their other cars, the lightweight all-alloy body of the V8 Vantage is hand-built in the company's shiny new headquarters at Gaydon in England. The Vantage is powered by Aston Martin's own 4.3-liter V8 engine — first used in the 1979 DBS V8 saloon — which delivers the relentless performance needed by the true supercar. The front mid-engined layout and the engine's low position within the body — achieved by combining it with a dry sump oil lubrication system — gives a low center of gravity so handling is agile and the car is well-balanced and easy to manage. Initially only a six-speed manual gearbox is available, but a paddle-shift automatic is on its way. The V8 is a high-performance car and offers the authentic sports car experience; inside the driver and passengers sit low and close to the road, to get what Aston Martin calls "a special sensation, usually only experienced in racing cars." The sumptuous interior features aluminum trim, hand-stitched leather and a choice of wood veneers.

| | |
|---|---|
| **ENGINE:** | Front mid-mounted, V8 |
| **CAPACITY:** | 4280 cc |
| **OUTPUT:** | 380 bhp @ 7300 rpm |
| **TOP SPEED:** | 175 mph |
| **ACCELERATION:** | 0–60 in 4.9 seconds |

# AUDI QUATTRO SPORT 1980

Audi, the last survivor of the great Auto Union and now a division of VW, has established a reputation for innovative design and superior engineering. The company's advertising slogan, Vorsprung Durch Technik (Progress through Technology) is probably the best-known German phrase in the non-German-speaking world and is well justified. Audi produced the first car to break the 400 kph barrier and Audis have taken the top three places at Le Mans. However, the five-cylinder engine – around which the original quattro was constructed – was a venerable diesel van unit, although its toughness and smooth running quickly won it admirers when coupled with the ingenious, permanent four-wheel-drive system from the VW Iltis military vehicle. The car's rally potential was very quickly recognized and exploited, notably by Hannu Mikkola and Stig Blomqvist, and its place in automotive history was assured. Production models offered turbocharging and ABS brakes and the name Quattro became synonymous with on-road four-wheel drive that offered enhanced performance and safety simultaneously.

| | | | |
|---|---|---|---|
| **ENGINE:** | Front-mounted, five cylinder, in line | **OUTPUT:** | 200 bhp @ 5500 rpm |
| | | **TOP SPEED:** | 137 mph |
| **CAPACITY:** | 2144 cc | **ACCELERATION:** | 0–60 in 7.1 seconds |

# AUSTIN-HEALEY 3000 1964

The Austin-Healey 3000 MkIII was the last in a line that defined the "hairy-chested" English sports car. This noble lineage began in 1952 with the unveiling of the Healey 100, powered by the Austin A90 Atlantic engine. Donald Healey had succeeded, against stiff opposition from MG and Jensen, in producing a sports car based on British Motor Corporation parts that appealed to Sir Leonard Lord, then head of BMC. Permission was duly granted for the cars to be produced at BMC's massive Longbridge works. Working in collaboration with his son, Geoffrey, Healey developed the car into a serious competitor both on the road and on the balance sheet. Works rally and racing versions were produced at MG's Abingdon factory and campaigned with tremendous success in events ranging from the Monte Carlo Rally to the Targa Florio. They were very fast and very noisy – and the cockpits got very hot – but it was every boy's idea of what a sports car ought to be. The final incarnation was fitted with an unburstable 3-liter, six-cylinder Austin lorry engine. Sadly, increasingly restrictive US legislation destroyed the Big Healeys' export market and production ceased in 1968.

| | | | |
|---|---|---|---|
| **ENGINE:** | Front-mounted, six cylinder in line | **OUTPUT:** | 148 bhp @ 5250 rpm |
| | | **TOP SPEED:** | 121 mph |
| **CAPACITY:** | 2912 cc | **ACCELERATION:** | 0–60 in 7.5 seconds |

# BENTLEY CONTINENTAL GT 2000

Despite efforts to revitalize a model range that represented little more than three decades of restyling and bolting-on, by the end of the nineties Bentley was but a shadow of the Silver Shadow. In 1997 Rolls-Royce Motor Cars was put up for sale by Rolls-Royce plc, the aero engine company that retained the rights to the use of the Rolls-Royce name and logo. BMW was eventually outbid by VW and the Bentley subsidiary of the Best Car in the World (with no name) – along with its works and its workforce with their incomparable expertise – passed into German hands for £430 million (over $700 million). BMW eventually got the Rolls-Royce name and badge, and nothing else, for £40 million (nearly $70 million). Project BY614 – the MSB (Medium Sized Bentley) – followed. This was a radical departure from previous practice at Crewe – at least since the glory days, which were recalled by Bentley's first win at Le Mans for over seventy years. Regardless of the fact that it shares its W-configured, twelve-cylinder engine with the incomprehensible VW Phaeton, the Continental GT is a motor of which W.O. Bentley would be immensely proud.

| | |
|---|---|
| **ENGINE:** | Front-mounted, W12 |
| **CAPACITY:** | 6000 cc |
| **OUTPUT:** | 552 bhp @ 6100 rpm |
| **TOP SPEED:** | 198 mph |
| **ACCELERATION:** | 0–60 in 4.7 seconds |

# BENTLEY R TYPE CONTINENTAL 1952

Rolls-Bentley (the companies had merged in 1931) had been developing a Grand Touring car before the outbreak of the Second World War. At the cessation of hostilities, the project – code-named Corniche – was resurrected but would now have to deliver a very different car for a very different world. Wartime austerity had fostered an understandable contempt for wastefulness and extravagance: the era of the Sedanca de Ville had passed. The new Bentley would have to combine restraint and efficiency with luxury and performance – and so it did. Developed from the somewhat banal MkVI of 1946, the R Type's 4.5-liter six-cylinder engine had its compression increased and its exhaust system reworked in order to provide sufficient power to propel the Continental prototype around the Le Mans circuit at an average speed of just under 120 mph over five laps. The "fastback" body, by H.J. Mulliner, struck exactly the right balance between form and function and thus the Bentley Continental contrived to be supremely elegant without displaying so much as a hint of vulgar excess.

| | |
|---|---|
| **ENGINE:** | Front-mounted, six cylinder in line |
| **CAPACITY:** | 4566 cc |
| **OUTPUT:** | 172 bhp |
| **TOP SPEED:** | 120 mph |
| **ACCELERATION:** | 0–60 in 13.0 seconds |

# BMW 2002 TURBO 1972

The BMW 2002 Turbo was Europe's first turbocharged road car. The KKK "blower" made its presence felt with a jolt at 4000 rpm and could power the glass-fiber-bodied coupé to fantastic speeds at a remarkable rate of acceleration. The sophisticated lowered suspension package was more than able to cope with the surging power output under most circumstances, but it cannot be denied that 2002 Turbo was an "exciting" car to drive. The white bodywork, with its "Go-Faster" stripes and stick-on spoilers – plus the emblazoning of the word turbo in mirror script on the front air dam – gave what was, in truth, a highly advanced performance car the look of a "Boy Racer" custom job. The interiors were Teutonically functional and the car was unhappy in urban environments. This, coupled with the oil crisis of 1973, served to restrict production to 1672 examples – making it rarer than the 507, if not quite so desirable.

| | |
|---|---|
| **ENGINE:** | Front-mounted, V8 |
| **CAPACITY:** | 3168 cc |
| **OUTPUT:** | 150 bhp @ 5000 rpm |
| **TOP SPEED:** | 125 mph |
| **ACCELERATION:** | 0–60 in 8.8 seconds |

# BMW 3.0 CSL 1973

BMW's elegant and sophisticated coupés epitomized seventies chic, though they were in fact bred out of a design that dated from the mid-sixties: the 2000CS. Despite sharing a platform with BMW's then somewhat uninspiring range of saloons, the Karmann-bodied coupés were dramatically styled and anticipated the cleaner, more angular look that was to characterize the decade. The CSLs (the "L" denoting "Lightweight") were the result of BMW's increasing interest in racing and were radically lightened and tuned for competition use. Factory cars, fitted with a 24-valve cylinder head, they were capable of producing more than 350 bhp. Later examples were fitted with massive rear spoilers to improve high-speed stability, and became known as "Batmobiles" because of their fantastic appearance. Striking looks were matched by staggering performance and the model's domination of its racing class was absolute. The CSL, along with its stable mates the CSA and the CSi, remained in production until the introduction of the "6 Series" coupés in 1975. They are still, however, highly desirable motor cars that are a delight to drive.

| | |
|---|---|
| **ENGINE:** | Front-mounted, six cylinder, in line |
| **CAPACITY:** | 3003 cc |
| **OUTPUT:** | 200 bhp @ 5500 rpm |
| **TOP SPEED:** | 140 mph |
| **ACCELERATION:** | 0–60 in 7.3 seconds |

# BMW 507 1956

Even though only 250 examples were manufactured, the 507 remains one of the most evocative cars ever produced by Bayerische Motoren Werke. It is one of the definitive roadsters, having its roots in the 501 saloon, which in turn was a development of BMW's pre-war 2-liter six-cylinder models. The arrival in 1954 of a beautifully engineered 2.5-liter V8, the first ever to be produced entirely in aluminum, paved the way for this masterpiece, which was styled by Count Albert Goetz. Goetz's studio was in New York, and in a complete departure from BMW's "house style" he produced a low-slung short-wheelbase sports car, whose appearance has influenced the look of such vehicles to this day. BMW's Z8 harks back to the fabulous fifties in its self-conscious references to the 507 – imitation being the sincerest form of flattery. But the 507's looks are pretty much unimprovable and its performance and handling were, in its day, equally impressive. Sadly, production was dilatory and the model was hugely expensive – more than twice the price of a Jaguar XK150 – and so the car never really caught on, especially with the vital American market.

| | | | |
|---|---|---|---|
| **ENGINE:** | Front-mounted, V8 | **TOP SPEED:** | 125 mph |
| **CAPACITY:** | 3168 cc | **ACCELERATION:** | 0–60 in 8.8 seconds |
| **OUTPUT:** | 150 bhp @ 5000 rpm | | |

# BMW M1 1978

The M1 is a true Cinderella, but although beautiful, capable, worthy and admirable, she never got to go to the ball. The car's antecedents were all of the highest order: styling was by Ital Design and was an object lesson in functional, elegant simplicity, molded in lightweight, incorruptible glass fiber. The construction of the car's complex, tubular chassis was entrusted initially to Lamborghini but was switched to Germany after unacceptable delays. By the time the car entered competition, which was self-evidently its primary purpose, it was already an aging design. Fond hopes of overtaking Porsche in Group 5 racing were never to be realized but, nonetheless, BMW produced a true supercar for the road. Power was supplied by the company's well-proven, 3.5-liter, six-cylinder engine as employed in the 635 CSi coupé, but fitted with a twin-cam four-valves-per-cylinder head that boosted output significantly. Four hundred road cars were produced, each one a thing of understated beauty that could deliver massive performance levels while maintaining perfect poise.

| | | | |
|---|---|---|---|
| **ENGINE:** | Mid-mounted, six cylinder, in line | **OUTPUT:** | 277 bhp @ 6500 rpm |
| | | **TOP SPEED:** | 165 mph |
| **CAPACITY:** | 3453 cc | **ACCELERATION:** | 0–60 in 5.6 seconds |

# BMW Z8 2000

The Z8 is an unashamed pastiche of BMW's seminal, fifties, 507 roadster. Like its illustrious predecessor, the Z8 was styled in the United States by a European – in this case Henrik Fischer, a Dane, working in California. The retro-styling conceals state-of-the-art construction: the aluminum, space-frame chassis is welded and glued together, by hand, in Germany. These cars are produced in extremely limited numbers, beautifully finished and fitted with the 5-liter V8 engine from the M5 saloon. The Z8 is hugely capable, refined and luxurious. Top speed is governed to 155 mph, but the car is capable of far more and so safety margins are considerable. Where the 507 pushed the boundaries, the Z8 sticks to the rules. It is a beautiful car, a fast car and a safe car, Some feel it's a car, for those – probably in their fifties – who remember the fifties and want to recapture some of the magic while sparing themselves the most exciting aspects of the period: noise, discomfort and danger!

| | |
|---|---|
| **ENGINE:** | Front-mounted, V8 |
| **CAPACITY:** | 4941 cc |
| **OUTPUT:** | 394 bhp @ 6600 rpm |
| **TOP SPEED:** | 155 mph |
| **ACCELERATION:** | 0–60 in 4.7 seconds |

# BRISTOL 411 1976

The Bristol is a magnificent anachronism. It is the automotive equivalent of the handmade suit: traditional, beautifully put together, eminently fit for its purpose and fitted precisely to the purchaser. A Bristol is for life. The 411 represented the ultimate expression of a design that dated from 1962, when the 407 was fitted with a Plymouth-Chrysler V8 in place of the pre-war BMW-derived six-cylinder engines that had powered Bristols since 1947. It is reported that Bristol's first cars, produced by an offshoot of the airplane company that had built the legendary Beau fighter, were fitted with engines "liberated" from Germany at the end of the war. Between 1969 and 1976 a mere 287 cars were produced in a succession of subtle variations on a well-proven theme. Engine capacity eventually rose to over 6.5 liters, causing some cooling problems in town driving, before a styling revision was matched with a "smaller" (5.9 liter) V8 fitted with a massive, Rotomaster turbocharger. The styling is deceptive; these cars are extremely potent and reward the "enthusiastic" driver richly.

| | |
|---|---|
| **ENGINE:** | Front-mounted, V8 |
| **CAPACITY:** | 6556 cc |
| **OUTPUT:** | 335 bhp @ 5200 rpm |
| **TOP SPEED:** | 140 mph |
| **ACCELERATION:** | 0–60 in 7.0 seconds |

# BRISTOL FIGHTER 2003

Bristol Cars are sold from a corner shop in London's Kensington High Street. The company has been in business, continuously, since the end of the Second World War and is one of Britain's last producers of genuine home-grown performance machinery. Having said that, Bristol has used American muscle to propel its elegant carriages since the sixties and the Fighter continues this tradition by employing the massive and magnificent aluminum V10 from Dodge's outrageous Viper. This engine was in turn developed from a commercial unit by Lamborghini in Italy. The Fighter's design – appropriately, considering its aeronautical heritage – is dictated purely by aerodynamics. It manages to combine the feel of a traditional sports car for the driver, while providing unsurpassed levels of luxury and refinement for the passengers. Anthony Crook's company, long the butt of jokes about "carriage clock" styling, has produced one of the most potent and practical supercars ever. An exclusive product for the discerning driver. Long may it thrive!

| | |
|---|---|
| **ENGINE:** | Front-mounted, V10 |
| **CAPACITY:** | 7990cc |
| **OUTPUT:** | 525 bhp @ 5100 rpm |
| **TOP SPEED:** | 210 mph |
| **ACCELERATION:** | 0–60 in 4.0 seconds |

# BUGATTI VEYRON 2006

Apart from its name, the Bugatti Veyron bears no relation whatsoever to the beautiful jewel-like machines built in the French province of Alsace between the wars. In 1998, Volkswagen purchased the Bugatti name, along with those of Bentley and Lamborghini. In the case of Bentley and Lamborghini, the cars, a factory and a workforce were part of the deal. Bugatti was but a dream. VW seem to have experienced some difficulty in turning this dream into a reality, a problem not simplified by the fact that, in whatever recognizable incarnation the Bugatti was resurrected, it would be in direct competition with one of VW's other "prestige" offerings: Bentley produce super-luxury coupés and sedans; Lamborghini produce state-of-the-art performance cars. The solution seems to have been to produce a car that is, above all else, extremely expensive. Though it is named for a legendary French racing driver, the Veyron is divinely decadent – some might say vulgar – and its (questionable) performance is irrelevant.

| | | | |
|---|---|---|---|
| **ENGINE:** | Mid-mounted, W16 | **TOP SPEED:** | 250 mph |
| **CAPACITY:** | 7993cc | **ACCELERATION:** | 0–60 in 3.0 seconds |
| **OUTPUT:** | 987 bhp @ 6000 rpm | | |

# BUICK ROADMASTER 1950

David Dunbar Buick entered the motor industry in 1899, having made a fortune out of creating the enamel bath tub. His company, based in Flint, Michigan, became the basis for the mighty General Motors Corporation, founded by Jimmy Durant in 1908. The "buck-toothed" Buick of 1950 marks a turning point in American automobile styling and design. Dynaflow automatic transmission was already in place, but the relaxed, venerable straight-8 engine was about to be replaced by a punchy oversquare V8 and those sumptuous forties curves were to give way to towering fins and acres of chromium plate. The Sedanette body, a fastback coupé style inherited from Cadillac, was to reappear in the splendid Continental Bentleys of the early fifties, but these cars are as American as apple pie. The Roadmaster is distinguished by the fact that it has four "ventiports" as opposed to the three sported by its lesser brethren in the Buick line. This styling quirk, introduced by Ned Nickles, was to become a Buick signature detail for nearly two decades.

| | | | |
|---|---|---|---|
| **ENGINE:** | Front-mounted, straight-8 | **TOP SPEED:** | 90 mph |
| **CAPACITY:** | 320.2 cu. in. | **ACCELERATION:** | 0–60 in 14.0 seconds |
| **OUTPUT:** | 150 bhp | | |

# CADILLAC ALLANTE 1987

The name Allanté is meaningless; it was derived from market research and believed to impart an impression of international sophistication. The Allanté was a remarkable project, either brave or foolhardy, depending on how you look at it, but ultimately – despite its apparent allure, with its Maserati-developed, turbocharged motor – it failed to win the hearts and minds of the American buying public. Based on a shortened version of the Eldorado platform, some of the Allanté's components crossed the Atlantic in both directions via the "Airbridge" – a specially adapted Boeing 747 that could carry 56 cars at a time between Detroit and Turin. Italian craftsmen at Pininfarina hand-built the bodies and fitted them onto the adapted subframes. The partially completed cars, fully painted and trimmed, were then flown back to GM's Hamtramck assembly plant, where the front-wheel-drive powertrain and suspension parts were fitted. The result: Italian style wedded to American muscle. How could it fail? Even though an Allanté paced the 76th Indianapolis 500 in 1993, its performance was never deemed sufficient to justify its price. The fitting of Cadillac's NorthStar V8 improved matters greatly, boosting top speed to 145 mph, but it was too late. Production ceased in 1993.

| | |
|---|---|
| **ENGINE:** | Front-mounted, V8 |
| **CAPACITY:** | 279 cu. in. |
| **OUTPUT:** | 295 bhp @ 5600 rpm |
| **TOP SPEED:** | 120 mph |
| **ACCELERATION:** | 0–60 in 9.5 seconds |

# CADILLAC ELDORADO 1953

The Golden One... 1953 was the Golden Dawn of America's love affair with the automobile, when it finally ceased to be practical transport and became an object of desire, a style statement and a status symbol. Owning an Eldorado had little to do with travel: it was about having arrived. Even Ike arrived in an Eldorado for his inauguration that year! Only 532 Eldos were built, all of them convertibles with a power-operated, disappearing hood. Power was increased by tweaking the '49 pattern V8's combustion chambers and valve gear, putting Cadillac on top of the heap once more. Legendary stylist Harley Earl insisted that the car be equipped with the world's first wrap-around windshield, even though each one had to be individually hand-formed. "Dagmars" appeared on the bumpers and the rear wings sprouted fins – the shape of things to come. Luxury equipment included dual-range Hydra-Matic automatic transmission and Saginaw power steering. The Eldorado was, and remains, a true Dream Machine. What seems odd is that this particular dream – from a time when gas was a few cents a gallon and always would be – rather than fading, seems to have returned. We all know that we should have grown out of fantasies like the Eldorado, but we haven't, have we?

| | |
|---|---|
| **Engine:** | Front-mounted, V8 |
| **Capacity:** | 331 cu. in. |
| **Output:** | 210 bhp @ 4150 rpm |
| **Top Speed:** | 120 mph |
| **Acceleration:** | 0–60 in 13.2 seconds |

# CATERHAM SEVEN 2006

The Caterham Seven is a little piece of motoring history. It dates back to the Lotus Seven of 1957, the car in which Formula One world champion Graham Hill began his racing career. Caterham Sevens are still built – in Caterham, Surrey, England – and they're still winning races. The latest, lightweight, CSR versions are powered by Ford Cosworth Duratec engines that develop substantial horsepower, but the Seven's super-stiff chassis and F1-style inboard suspension, mated to 15-inch Avon tires, is more than able to cope. These cars represent just about the ultimate driving experience and are definitely not for the faint-hearted or lovers of creature comforts. They are designed to be quick, fast and – in competent hands – safe. Graham Nearn's Caterham Cars took over production of the Seven in the seventies and the company has developed it continually for three decades. What is truly remarkable is that the Seven just gets better and better and better – there seems no end in sight. If you're looking for a car that can hit sixty miles an hour from rest in three seconds, it is worth bearing in mind that the Caterham Seven is considerably cheaper than the Bugatti Veyron.

| | |
|---|---|
| **ENGINE:** | Front-mounted, four cylinder |
| **CAPACITY:** | 2.3 liters |
| **OUTPUT:** | 260 bhp @ 7500 rpm |
| **TOP SPEED:** | 155 mph |
| **ACCELERATION:** | 0–60 in 3.1 seconds |

# CHEVROLET CORVETTE 1953

The Corvette is the American sports car. It was born out of a desire to provide young Americans, many of whom had seen action in Europe in the Second World War, with something to rival the Jaguars and MGs that they'd got to know "across the pond." The original car, brainchild of the ever-inventive Harley Earl and engineered by the equally resourceful Ed Cole, was produced (in Polo White only) in a corner of GM's massive plant at Flint, Michigan. It was powered by an upgraded, Chevrolet truck motor (the "Stovebolt Six") that dated from 1927, had two-speed Powerglide transmission, ran on bus tires and sported the world's first volume-produced fiberglass bodywork, formed from 46 separate pieces. The Corvette was named for a fast, maneuverable vessel, but it was neither fast nor maneuverable and with its creaking, leaking bodywork, pram hood and side-screens, it wasn't too comfortable either – and it was expensive! It did, however, have some style, and even vestigial fins! Crude as it was, the Corvette somehow captured America's spirit and has continued to do so ever since.

| | |
|---|---|
| **Engine:** | Front-mounted, six cylinder |
| **Capacity:** | 235 cu. in. |
| **Output:** | 150 bhp @ 4500 rpm |
| **Top Speed:** | 110 mph |
| **Acceleration:** | 0–60 in 11.0 seconds |

# CHEVROLET CORVETTE C6 Z06 2006

The 2005 C6 Corvette was the first model to feature exposed headlights since 1962. The 2006 Z06 is the fastest and most powerful Corvette ever built. Once more a 427 cu. in. block was fitted and once more the venerable 'Vette was ready to take on all comers. This is a true supercar, with handling and safety features concomitant with the car's truly awesome performance – yet its overall fuel consumption is 22.6 miles per gallon. That's impressive for a 7-liter engine; the Ferrari Modena, by comparison, can only manage 12.7 mpg for the same power output. The car's body is not made from glass fiber, in the Corvette tradition, but is crafted from aluminum, its fenders and hood being formed in carbon fiber. The chassis cradle is of magnesium and the engine's con-rods and inlet valves are titanium. All this combines to give a weight of less than 3200 lb. The interior has lightweight seats that are designed to hold the driver (and, hopefully, the passenger) firmly in place under the fighter-plane G forces that can be generated in fast cornering. Dave Hill, Corvette's chief engineer, has stated "Our goal is to create a Corvette that does more things well than any other performance car." And there you have it.

| | |
|---|---|
| **ENGINE:** | Front-mounted, V8 |
| **CAPACITY:** | 427 cu. in. |
| **OUTPUT:** | 505 bhp @ 6200 rpm |
| **TOP SPEED:** | 195 mph |
| **ACCELERATION:** | 0–60 in 3.7 seconds |

# CHEVROLET
# CORVETTE ROADSTER 1986

The original Corvette was – all too literally – a ragtop, and a full convertible continued to be offered from 1953 until 1975, when safety fears finally brought about its deletion. Happily, the Roadster returned in 1986. No Corvettes at all were built in 1983, but the following year an all-new model was announced. This was the work of engineer Dave McLellan and stylist Jerry Palmer and it contrived to combine safety, strength, sophistication and style while still being instantly recognizable as a 'Vette. The L-83 version of the venerable 350 cu. in. "small block" V8 featured computer-controlled Cross-Fire fuel injection and was mated to a sophisticated aluminum "backbone" chassis. A complex and unwieldy "4+3" manual transmission system, designed to improve fuel economy by (firmly) encouraging the driver to avoid intermediate gears, was soon dropped and Cross-Fire gave way to Tuned Port injection which, coupled with increased compression, provided an additional 25 bhp. Bosch anti-lock ABS brakes became standard and "handed" wheels and tires (that could only be fitted to the correct side of the car) were introduced to provide handling and road holding that were a match for any European competition.

| | | | |
|---|---|---|---|
| **ENGINE:** | Front-mounted, V8 | **TOP SPEED:** | 140 mph |
| **CAPACITY:** | 350 cu. in. | **ACCELERATION:** | 0–60 in 6.5 seconds |
| **OUTPUT:** | 230 bhp @ 4300 rpm | | |

# CHEVROLET CORVETTE STING RAY 1966

Bill Mitchell's eye-popping new Corvette debuted in 1963, sporting a completely new body with concealed headlights and (on the coupé) a divided rear window that was to be deleted after the first year of production – thus producing an instant collector's classic. Zora Arkus-Duntov designed a ladder-frame chassis that allowed the new car to sit lower on the road and provided near-perfect weight distribution. Fitted with the Turbo Fire 327 V8, performance was incredible and racing success followed almost immediately. A massive 427 "big block" engine was offered as an option and many later examples sported power-bulges and "sidewinder" exhausts – neither of which really suited what was an exceptionally handsome and, by American standards, restrained design. 1966 should have been the Sting Ray's last year but production problems with its replacement allowed it a brief Indian summer in 1967, by which time exterior embellishments had been effectively eliminated. Unusually, the Sting Ray's styling got simpler, and better, as it got older.

| | | | |
|---|---|---|---|
| **ENGINE:** | Front-mounted, V8 | **TOP SPEED:** | 140 mph |
| **CAPACITY:** | 427 cu. in. | **ACCELERATION:** | 0–60 in 4.8 seconds |
| **OUTPUT:** | 450 bhp | | |

# CHEVROLET CORVETTE ZR1 1990

The defining feature of Corvette's King of the Hill was its Lotus-designed quad-cam 32-valve, all-alloy V8 engine, designated the LT5. The engine block was produced deep in the heart of Texas and the sump was made in Missouri, but the cylinder head came from England, along with the crankshaft and con-rods, and the pistons and cylinder liners were made in Germany. The engines were assembled by Mercury Marine of Stillwater, Oklahoma and the whole thing finally rolled out of the factory at Bowling Green, Kentucky. When it finally came together, the ZR1 was magnificent. Performance was so impressive that a "valet key" was supplied to prevent the unwary from unleashing the ferocious power of the engine unwittingly. This restricted output to a mere 240 bhp! By the time production ceased, output had crept up to over 400 bhp. First gear could take the car to 56 mph while sixth provided cruising at 42 mph per 1000 rpm. Had the engine been capable of pulling maximum revs in sixth gear, top speed would have exceeded 300 mph! The ZR1 was the most expensive Corvette ever produced, by a margin of some $20,000, but it was still less than half the price of a Ferrari Testarossa – with similar performance.

| | | | |
|---|---|---|---|
| **ENGINE:** | Front-mounted, V8 | **TOP SPEED:** | 175 mph |
| **CAPACITY:** | 350 cu. in. | **ACCELERATION:** | 0–60 in 4.5 seconds |
| **OUTPUT:** | 380 bhp @ 6200 rpm | | |

# CHRYSLER 300C 2005

The merging of Daimler-Benz and Chrysler – two venerable giants of the motor industry – is resulting in some interesting and exciting machinery, which is already beginning to call into question the long and fondly held European view that anything even remotely linked to Detroit must be a gas-guzzling wallow-box. The 300C can give a lot of European saloons a good run for their money, not only in terms of performance but in sheer value-for-money. The Chrysler delivers an awful lot of bangs for not a lot of bucks. Top power plant option is, appropriately, a big V8 "Hemi" recalling the glory days of the model's illustrious 1955 predecessor. The traditional front-engine-rear-drive setup (four-wheel drive is an optional extra) provides excellent handling for a big saloon – and the 300C is a big saloon. Though the car's styling may strike many Europeans as brash, inside the levels of equipment and comfort are extremely impressive and the list of luxury options is huge. A system that allows the engine to run on four cylinders instead of eight when circumstances allow provides fuel economy that, for a big V8, is very good indeed.

| | | | |
|---|---|---|---|
| **ENGINE:** | Front-mounted, V8 | **TOP SPEED:** | 155 mph |
| **CAPACITY:** | 5.7 liters | **ACCELERATION:** | 0–60 in. 6.4 seconds |
| **OUTPUT:** | 340 bhp @ 5000 rpm | | |

# CHRYSLER C-300 1955

The original Chrysler 300 took its title from the fact that the cast iron, FirePower V8 – with its legendary, hemispherical combustion chambers – that powered it developed 300 horsepower. As with the latest Chrysler 300s, the 1955 represented a big turnaround in the company's fortunes – sales jumped by 50 percent over the previous year's figures. The car was styled, perhaps a little hesitantly, by Virgil Exner. Up front, the radiator grille was borrowed from the Chrysler Imperial, and at the rear the fins look distinctly like an afterthought. Things were to improve in this department, however, and the engineering, courtesy of Robert M. Roger, exuded confidence from the start. Breathing through twin, four-barrel carburetors and fitted with the obligatory "knobbly cam" and high (8.5 to 1) compression head, the C-300 quickly established a reputation on the track as well as on the street: Tim Flock drove one to victory at Daytona two years running. The C-300 was Chrysler's response to GM's Corvette and Ford's Thunderbird, but owed nothing to either in terms of styling or character – it had a powerful personality of its own.

| | |
|---|---|
| **ENGINE:** | Front-mounted, V8 |
| **CAPACITY:** | 331 cu. in. |
| **OUTPUT:** | 300 bhp @ 5200 rpm |
| **TOP SPEED:** | 127 mph |
| **ACCELERATION:** | 0–60 in 9.5 seconds |

# CISITALIA 202 GRAN SPORT 1948

The first thing that strikes one about this Italian classic is its classic Italian styling. The Cisitalia coupé is the work of Pininfarina and was the car that established his company's international reputation. Elegant and purposeful, the Cisitalia exuded confidence and style – rare qualities in a European car in the immediate post-war years. The first cars from Piero Dusio's Turin factory were powered by tiny 1100 cc Fiat motors and were intended for racing! Extensive wind-tunnel testing produced some extremely handsome and efficient designs, culminating in Pininfarina's coupé (actually built by Vignale), which is generally regarded as the definitive example of the breed. Low weight helped the car to attain speeds as great as, if not a little greater than, cars with far larger engines; a 60 hp variant was capable of over 100 mph. In 1951 a Cisitalia was placed on show at the New York Museum of Modern Art. Sadly, Signor Dusio seemed to lose interest in the car, being more concerned with developing Grand Prix racers, and production ceased in 1953 after fewer than 200 examples had been completed.

| | |
|---|---|
| **ENGINE:** | Front-mounted, four cylinder |
| **CAPACITY:** | 1089 cc |
| **OUTPUT:** | 55 bhp @ 5500 rpm |
| **TOP SPEED:** | 99 mph |
| **ACCELERATION:** | 0–60 Not Available |

# CITROËN SM 1970

The Citroën SM was an ambitious and innovative project whose success was stifled by the oil crisis of 1973. Citroën had taken on prestigious but penniless Maserati in the late sixties and pressed ahead bravely with a hybrid design intended to combine luxury and performance and re-establish its Gallic supremacy. Instead, it ended in Citroën itself being taken over by its arch-rival Peugeot. Because of France's engine-capacity-based taxation system, a six-cylinder unit displacing just less than 2.8 liters (the tax break) was produced, later to find its way into an appealing mid-engined Maserati coupé, the Merak. One can only ponder on the car that might have resulted from the use of Maserati's magnificent 4.7 liter V8, but even with its "baby-boomer" engine, Citroën's renowned hydraulics and aerodynamic styling combined to produce what is probably the last of the Grand Routiers. Despite its Italian power plant, the traction-avant SM remains an essentially, exquisitely, French car: elegant and complex as fine claret and just as rewarding to the connoisseur.

| ENGINE: | Front-mounted, V6 |
|---|---|
| CAPACITY: | 2670 cc |
| OUTPUT: | 180 bhp @ 6250 rpm |
| TOP SPEED: | 135 mph |
| ACCELERATION: | 0–60 in 9.0 seconds |

# DAIMLER DOUBLE SIX 1972

The Double Six Daimler was in fact nothing more than a Jaguar XJ12 with a fluted radiator shell and a nicer trim, but its name recalled the glory days of one of the great names in motoring history. Rumors of Jaguar's new V12 had circulated for years and expectations ran high, especially after the showing of the gorgeous Bertone-bodied Pirana prototype, sponsored by the *Daily Telegraph* newspaper, which eventually became the Lamborghini Espada. What finally arrived was not quite so exciting. The engine had single camshafts and hydraulic valve gear and was connected to a three-speed automatic gearbox. Power output was less than that of a 3.8-liter E-Type but fuel consumption was monumental – an average of 12 mpg! In its favor, the car was extremely luxurious and civilized, and the Daimler versions were finished to a very high standard. Power delivery was turbine smooth and the car would cruise effortlessly at well over 100 mph, but its thirst, especially during the oil crisis of the early seventies, was its undoing. Given a V12 power plant, William Lyons – the Lyon behind every Jaguar, at least until the merger with BMC – would have produced something quite spectacular. British Leyland didn't.

| | |
|---|---|
| **ENGINE:** | Front-mounted, V12 |
| **CAPACITY:** | 5343 cc |
| **OUTPUT:** | 250 bhp @ 6000 rpm |
| **TOP SPEED:** | 140 mph |
| **ACCELERATION:** | 0–60 in 7.4 seconds |

# DAIMLER SP 250/DART 1959

The Daimler Dart was a radical departure from standard Daimler practice. The company's reputation was based firmly on its luxury saloons and limousines: cars with names like Majestic and Conquest – cars fit for kings! A number of rakish roadsters had been produced between the wars, however, including the magnificent V12 "Double Six." The Dart was the last of this elusive and illustrious line and combined innovation with tradition in a heady little cocktail. The body, a peculiar mixture of curves and corners, was made from glass fiber panels and mounted on a chassis that lacked the necessary torsional rigidity to prevent the doors opening during hard cornering. At the heart of the Dart was a gem of an engine: a jewel-like 2.5-liter V8 designed by Edward Turner. The 4.5-liter version of this engine, as fitted to the massive Majestic Major saloon, gave 100 mph cruising in a car that had all the aerodynamic efficiency of a garden shed. Daimler was swallowed up by Jaguar in 1961 and the Dart was discontinued. The V8 engine lived on, briefly, in the Daimler equivalent of the Jaguar MkII, the 250.

| | |
|---|---|
| **ENGINE:** | Front-mounted, V8 |
| **CAPACITY:** | 2547 cc |
| **OUTPUT:** | 140 bhp @ 5800 rpm |
| **TOP SPEED:** | 123 mph |
| **ACCELERATION:** | 0–60 in 7.4 seconds |

# DATSUN 240Z 1969

Blinded by the rising sun, MG lost its position as the manufacturer of the world's most popular sports car (the MGB) to the Datsun 240Z in the early seventies. This is precisely what the 240Z was designed to achieve and it isn't too hard to see how it did it. Power was originally to have been supplied by a Jaguar-inspired engine with twin overhead camshafts, but development proved costly and troublesome and the project almost foundered. However, Toyota's entry into the sports car lists with the 2000 GT prodded Datsun back into action and an excellent, far simpler single-cam six-cylinder power plant was produced. This was fitted into a very European-looking coupé body designed by none other than Count Albert Goetz, who had been responsible for BMW's ravishing fifties Roadster, the 507. The shape was somewhere between the Jaguar E-Type and the Ferrari Daytona so the car was not unattractive to look upon. Performance was exhilarating; sophisticated suspension and rack-and-pinion steering allowed the car to be "chucked about" in the finest European tradition and the whole package exuded masculine muscularity.

| | |
|---|---|
| **ENGINE:** | Front-mounted, six cylinder |
| **CAPACITY:** | 2393 cc |
| **OUTPUT:** | 151 bhp @ 5600 rpm |
| **TOP SPEED:** | 125 mph |
| **ACCELERATION:** | 0–60 in 8.0 seconds |

# DeLOREAN DMC 12 1981

The DeLorean could have been designed by Karl Marx to demonstrate the inherent flaws in the capitalist system. It was conceived out of personal greed, corporate corruption and executive deceit. Ideology aside, the DMC 12 remains a strange beast by any standards. The son of a Ford factory worker, John Zachary DeLorean had enjoyed a meteoric rise to corporate stardom at General Motors where, during his tenure at Pontiac, he became the father of the legendary GTO. In 1973, seemingly on impulse, he abandoned Detroit, Michigan, for Dunmurry in Northern Ireland. Here, with $12m gleaned from individual investors and $156m in grants from the British government, he proceeded to turn his dream into a nightmare. Giugiaro was put in charge of styling and Lotus hired to handle the engineering, but the backbone-chassised, gullwing-doored, stainless-steel-bodied juggernaut that finally lumbered forth was (under)powered by a Renault V6, mounted in the tail. Everything about the car was wrong: weight distribution, finish, handling, performance and price. Eight thousand cars were completed before the company collapsed. With leaden irony, the time-travelling vehicle in the film *Back to the Future* was based on a DeLorean.

| | |
|---|---|
| **Engine:** | Rear-mounted, V6 |
| **Capacity:** | 2393 cc |
| **Output:** | 132 bhp @ 5500 rpm |
| **Top Speed:** | 109 mph |
| **Acceleration:** | 0–60 in 10.5 seconds |

# DE TOMASO PANTERA GTS 1973

Alejandro de Tomaso was an Argentinian who emigrated to Italy in the hope of emulating his illustrious compatriots of earlier years: Mieres, Gonzales and the immortal Fangio. He ended up taking on the giants of Modena – Lamborghini, Maserati and Ferrari – at their own game and making a pretty good job of it. The Pantera was a hybrid: Italian chassis/American engine. The motor was a 5.7-liter, Ford "Cleveland" unit. Apart from its high-compression (11:1) head, it was a very conventional unit or, to put it another way, a highly reliable unit. It delivered maximum power with minimal fuss. The idea was to put these elegant items (styled by Tom Tjaarda of Ghia, a Ford subsidiary) in Ford showrooms across the United States to tempt Corvette buyers away from GM – and it might have succeeded but for the seventies oil crisis and the innate conservatism of American motorists. On the road, the Pantera is a very convincing car. It pulls like a train, handles nimbly and cruises effortlessly. One is reduced to looking for trouble: the big, four-barrel carb can get caught out in hard cornering, causing impressive misfire, and the driving position is pretty bizarre, even by Italian standards, but overall, this is a cool car.

| | |
|---|---|
| **ENGINE:** | Rear-mounted, V8 |
| **CAPACITY:** | 5763 cc |
| **OUTPUT:** | 350 bhp @ 6000 rpm |
| **TOP SPEED:** | 160 mph |
| **ACCELERATION:** | 0–60 in 5.5 seconds |

# DODGE VIPER 1992

The Dodge Viper parallels the development of the Corvette ZR1, save that whereas Chevrolet went looking for inspiration in England, Dodge turned to Italy. Even so, the mechanical masterpiece that Lamborghini produced to power this off-the-shelf hot rod had itself started out in the States: the V10 engine was derived from a Chrysler commercial vehicle unit. To say that the Viper – whose name is obviously intended to conjure images of the Cobra, and in whose creation Carroll Shelby himself took a hand – is powered by a truck engine, however, is not even close to being accurate. The Viper's V10 provides neck-wrenching acceleration on the open road while being utterly docile in traffic. It's "back-to-basics" image – originals had clip-on side curtains reminiscent of the first Corvettes! – concealed immense sophistication: the bodywork being a composite structure of steel and GRP, mounted on a totally unyielding tubular chassis. Later versions of the Viper – the GTS, the RT-10 and the GTS/R – have taken performance levels even higher with capacity increasing to over 500 cu. in. and output topping 600 bhp.

| | |
|---|---|
| **ENGINE:** | Front-mounted, V10 |
| **CAPACITY:** | 488 cu. in. |
| **OUTPUT:** | 400 bhp @ 4600 rpm |
| **TOP SPEED:** | 165 mph |
| **ACCELERATION:** | 0–60 in 4.5 seconds |

# EXCALIBUR SS 1966

Named for the legendary King Arthur's legendary sword, the original Excalibur SS had all the finesse of a battle-ax. It was the brainchild of Brooks Stevens, an industrial designer who by 1963 had worked with both Henry J. and Kaiser-Fraser. Charged with producing a "show-stopper" to entice potential purchasers onto the stand of the ailing Studebaker concern at the 1964 New York Auto Show, Stevens delivered the Studebaker SS. The car was a pastiche of the legendary pre-war Mercedes SSK, powered by a 290 hp Studebaker V8 and cobbled together by Stevens and his two sons in six weeks. Studebaker got cold feet and backed out of the idea; the company subsequently collapsed. Stevens registered the name Excalibur and soldiered on alone; he subsequently prospered. The 1966 SS was powered by a "small block" 327 Chevrolet V8 in Corvette tune. This motor, mounted in Stevens' rigid-chassis retro-styled cycle-winged contraption, provided blistering performance. Stevens had found himself a niche market, and although later examples of the marque tended toward show rather than go, the original Excalibur SS was a fast and furious one-of-a-kind.

| | |
|---|---|
| **ENGINE:** | Front-mounted, V8 |
| **CAPACITY:** | 327 cu. in. |
| **OUTPUT:** | 300 bhp @ 6000 rpm |
| **TOP SPEED:** | 150 mph |
| **ACCELERATION:** | 0–60 in 4.8 seconds |

# FACEL VEGA HK500 1960

FACEL, like FIAT, is an acronym: Forges et Ateliers de Construction d'Eure et Loire was the coach-building concern of Jean Daninos. With the decline in demand for bespoke bodywork, Daninos decided to produce a car of his own – the Vega, named for a star. Introduced to the world at the Paris Salon of 1954, the Facel Vega was fast, powered by a Chrysler/De Soto FireDome V8, but it was above all sumptuous. The body, with its stacked headlights and wrap-around glass, was positively futuristic and attention to detail extended to stainless steel brightwork instead of chromium plate. The interior was beautifully appointed and equally innovative, with the minor instruments grouped in a central console rather than scattered at random across the dashboard. The Achilles heel of early models was their fade-prone drum brakes but disks were introduced in 1960. By modern standards, the Facel's handling would be judged appalling, but in its day it was manageable, particularly in the hands of an enthusiast.

| | | | |
|---|---|---|---|
| **ENGINE:** | Front-mounted, V8 | **TOP SPEED:** | 145 mph |
| **CAPACITY:** | 5910 cc | **ACCELERATION:** | 0–60 in 8.5 seconds |
| **OUTPUT:** | 360 bhp @ 5200 rpm | | |

# FERRARI 365 GTB/4 DAYTONA 1968

The first generation of V12 Berlinetta Ferraris culminated with the 365 GTB/4. Unveiled at the Paris Motor Show in 1968, the car was christened to celebrate Ferrari's famous victory in the 24-hour race at Daytona the previous year. The gorgeous bodywork was styled by Pininfarina and built, in Modena, by Scaglietti. Although only a two-seater – there was no infantile 2+2 rear accommodation – the Daytona was a big, heavy car, tipping the scales at 3600 lb, and it required a big, heavy driver to control it. Power from the quad-cam V12 was doled out in great lumps rather than smooth, even servings, and even with all-independent suspension and a trans-axle gearbox to improve weight distribution, it was all too easy to get the Daytona sideways. The days of the docile boulevard-cruiser from Modena were still in the future; the Daytona was a car designed to be driven hard by hard drivers and its competition success bears witness to this. Racing versions could put out 450 bhp and could approach 200 mph, leading to a class win at Le Mans in 1973.

| | | | |
|---|---|---|---|
| **ENGINE:** | Front-mounted, V12 | **TOP SPEED:** | 174 mph |
| **CAPACITY:** | 4390 cc | **ACCELERATION:** | 0–60 in 5.4 seconds |
| **OUTPUT:** | 352 bhp @ 7500 rpm | | |

# FERRARI DINO 246GT 1973

The Dino, Ferrari's first mid-engined road car, was named in honour of Enzo Ferrari's son, who died in 1956 at the age of 24. It is perhaps the most perfect example of the "young man's car" ever built, combining style and romance with incomparable joie de vivre. Although modestly priced by Modena standards, a young man would have had to be very well-off to buy one of these beauties in 1973 – the cost was roughly that of two E-Type Jaguars, but it was worth every cent. Styling was by Pininfarina but the bodies were built by Scaglietti. The cast-iron block (early, 206 Dinos had aluminum engines) was centrally mounted, giving perfect weight distribution that resulted in impeccable road manners. Subtle suspension, combined with a slick, five-speed gearbox, invited spirited driving. The Dino was a car that belonged on the long and winding road, not on the motorway or the boulevard. Adding together 206s and 246s, coupés and Spiders, over 4000 Dinos were produced between 1967 and 1974. The beautiful, V6 engine lived on in the Fiat Dino and the Lancia Stratos until 1975.

| | |
|---|---|
| **ENGINE:** | Mid-mounted, V6 |
| **CAPACITY:** | 2418 cc |
| **OUTPUT:** | 195 bhp @ 7600 rpm |
| **TOP SPEED:** | 150 mph |
| **ACCELERATION:** | 0–60 in 7.0 seconds |

# FERRARI ENZO 2003

Announced at the 2002 Paris Motor Show, the Enzo is the latest in a distinguished line of limited edition machines such as the GTO, the F40 and the F50. Initially 349 examples were to be built, but this was increased to 399 because of the demand for this $650,000 runaround. Named after Il Commendatore himself, the Enzo is effectively a competition car adapted (just) for road use. The nose section, clearly influenced by F1 practice, gives the Enzo a slightly kit-car look but this is a machine intended for driving rather than dalliance and it is to be hoped that the lucky few who have secured one will make use of their investment rather than keeping it locked away – "used" examples are worth well over $1m already. The Enzo's incredible aerodynamics supply massive downforce with minimal drag, making it the fastest road-going Ferrari ever produced – the speedometer reads to 250 mph. Each purchaser is invited to the factory to have the car individually tailored to their personal measurements and specific requirements and the pedals can be adjusted for those who favor left-foot braking.

| | |
|---|---|
| **ENGINE:** | Mid-mounted, V12 |
| **CAPACITY:** | 5988 cc |
| **OUTPUT:** | 660 bhp @ 7800 rpm |
| **TOP SPEED:** | 225 mph |
| **ACCELERATION:** | 0–60 in 3.6 seconds |

# FERRARI F40
# 1987

If the Ferrari F40 were a movie, it would be at the same time "art house" and "high concept." Built to celebrate 40 glorious years of production at Modena, the F40 was supposed to have been a limited edition of 450 units. Such was the excitement – and demand – created that 1311 cars were eventually built. Based on the 288 GTO platform, the F40 was powered by a comparatively small (under 3 liters) V8, but twin turbochargers enabled this unit to produce close to 500 bhp. Lightweight materials such as Kevlar and carbon fiber were used in its construction, drawing on Ferrari's incomparable F1 experience. For all its beauty, the F40 was a spartan machine, eschewing creature comforts in favor of raw performance. At speed, the sound level in the cockpit made conversation impossible, but the noise was magnificent and the driver was (hopefully) concentrating on driving. Styling was by Pininfarina but the F40's body was assembled "in house" by Ferrari. The F40 was the last car bearing his name that Enzo Ferrari lived to see produced. It was a fitting finale: the fastest production car on earth.

| | |
|---|---|
| **Engine:** | Mid-mounted, V8 |
| **Capacity:** | 2936 cc |
| **Output:** | 478 bhp @ 7000 rpm |
| **Top Speed:** | 201 mph |
| **Acceleration:** | 0–60 in 4.7 seconds |

# FERRARI 612 SCAGLIETTI 2006

Replacing the 456M, the 612 Scaglietti – named for the renowned stylist Sergio Scaglietti – has both an aluminum frame and aluminum panels. It is at once a traditional Ferrari road car, having a front-mounted V12 engine driving the rear wheels, and at the same time a state-of-the-art supercar with staggering performance levels. Transmission is via a six-speed sequential gearbox operated via "paddle" shifters either side of the wheel – though a stick shift may be ordered as an option. The transmission may be switched into automatic mode for more relaxed driving – not that the 612 invites relaxed driving. The rear seats are little more than decorative but the front ones are extremely practical, encouraging all-day driving for the sheer pleasure of it – a very rare sensation in this day and age. Even at a list price of $250,000, the 612 was sold out for eighteen months at its launch. Such prices for cars may be considered obscene but the 612 is one of the very, very few that just about justifies its cost. Even by Ferrari's exacting standards, the 612 is a beautiful, beautifully engineered car that is beautiful to drive. Styling, incidentally, is by Pininfarina.

| | |
|---|---|
| **ENGINE:** | Front-mounted, V12 |
| **CAPACITY:** | 5748 cc |
| **OUTPUT:** | 540 bhp @ 7250 rpm |
| **TOP SPEED:** | 195 mph |
| **ACCELERATION:** | 0–60 in 4.2 seconds |

# FERRARI TESTAROSSA 1984

The Testarossa ("Redhead") takes its name from its scarlet valve covers and harks back to early racing success. As much an exercise in style as in function, the Testarossa set out to be strikingly beautiful and succeeded in its aim. The body is "sculpted" – the delicate "cooling" fins that adorn the side vents do no more than that, but they help to give an impression of speed even when the car is standing still. Developed from the excellent 512BB, the Testarossa's engine layout featured two banks of six cylinders, horizontally opposed. This design seems to produce an almost gyroscopic effect as drivers of Alfa Sud GTis will testify. The main problem with driving the Testarossa was its sheer size. In photographs it looks as compact as a Dino, but it was, in fact, 6 feet 6 inches wide. Despite this, the car was light to drive, agile and extremely tractable – more so than its predecessor. Acceleration and road holding were tremendous; the Testarossa could pass just about anything on the road, but one had to be sure that there was room to pass!

| | |
|---|---|
| **ENGINE:** | Mid-mounted, Flat 12 |
| **CAPACITY:** | 4942 cc |
| **OUTPUT:** | 390 bhp @ 6300 rpm |
| **TOP SPEED:** | 180 mph |
| **ACCELERATION:** | 0–60 in 5.6 seconds |

# FIAT 8V 1952

The Fiat 8V was the company's first post-war sports car. It was christened the 8V because the Ford Motor Corporation had exclusive rights to the term V8 at the time. Fiat's chief engineer, Dante Giacosa, had designed a very tidy and compact alloy 2-liter unit for a proposed sedan that never went into production. Primarily intended for competition, the 8Vs were prepared at SIATA in Turin. Bodywork was on the *superleggera* pattern – light paneling over a tubular frame – and was initially styled by Rapi. Later, other coach-builders, including Ghia, Vignale and Zagato, produced bodies for the 8V, some of them extremely handsome. Similarly, the engine was available in various states of tune, depending on the customer's intentions. A number of other interesting variants appeared, including a glass-fiber-bodied example, shown at Geneva in 1954, and an experimental, gas-turbine-powered version. Despite the car's beauty and its competition success, fewer than 120 cars were ever built before production ceased at the end of 1954.

| | | | |
|---|---|---|---|
| **ENGINE:** | Front-mounted, V8 | **TOP SPEED:** | 120 mph |
| **CAPACITY:** | 1996 cc | **ACCELERATION:** | 0–60 in 12.3 seconds |
| **OUTPUT:** | 105 bhp @ 6000 rpm | | |

# FIAT DINO 1969

The Dino, named after Enzo Ferrari's son who had died in 1956, was originally intended to become an independent range of cars fitted with the Ferrari V6 engine. In its first form, this had an aluminum block and displaced 2.0 liters, but later versions were made in cast iron and their capacity increased to 2.4 liters. Ferrari Dinos (the GT version) carry the famous "prancing horse" badge but are not actually badged as Ferraris. Fiat – which built the Spiders and coupés – had long been a close associate of Ferrari and was unable to resist the temptation to exploit this link; so Turin-made cars are badged as Fiats. The Fiats have long been regarded as the poor relation but this is grossly unfair. The Ferrari (GT) version is fabulous, of course, but the Fiats have a beauty all their own and the understated Bertone-styled coupés are particularly attractive, if only for their ability to surprise Jaguar drivers at the lights. The Pininfarina Spiders are outrageous and immense fun in the sun – or beneath the stars. Both benefit from a robust, five-speed ZF gearbox that encourages spirited driving.

| | | | |
|---|---|---|---|
| **ENGINE:** | Front-mounted, V6 | **TOP SPEED:** | 130 mph |
| **CAPACITY:** | 2418 cc | **ACCELERATION:** | 0–60 in 7.5 seconds |
| **OUTPUT:** | 180 bhp @ 6600 rpm | | |

# FORD GALAXIE 500 1965

Fords in the sixties were graded by size and the Galaxie was big, in every sense. Emanating from the Fairlane series, the name Galaxie was first applied to Sunliner convertibles and Skyliner retractables in 1959. At a time of recession, the Big Three – Ford, GM and Chrysler – were in fierce competition for dwindling sales and a new range of Galaxie pillarless sedans caused a major stir. In the mid-sixties the Galaxie 500, massive as it was, became firmly established as a competition car. A team of these behemoths was brought to England and provided spectators at Brands Hatch with some of the most exciting saloon-car racing ever, mixing it mightily with competition that included MkII Jaguars and Mini Coopers. These cars rode a wheel-base of almost 10 feet and weighed well over 3000 lb, though some racing versions were fiberglass-bodied. Engines could be optioned up to a 427 (7 liter) V8 and tuned to produce in excess of 500 hp. On the track they wallowed horribly through bends but could certainly burn up the straights. We shall not see their like again – in the 1960s Galaxies moved people, now they're People Movers.

| | |
|---|---|
| **ENGINE:** | Front-mounted, V8 |
| **CAPACITY:** | 427 cu. in. |
| **OUTPUT:** | 425 bhp @ 6000 rpm |
| **TOP SPEED:** | 140 mph |
| **ACCELERATION:** | 0–60 in 6.5 seconds |

# FORD GT40 1965

While Ford's monstrous Galaxie 500 was dominating  stock car racing in the United States and saloon car racing in Europe, the remarkable GT40 set out to snatch one of the most prestigious prizes in all of motor sport by winning the Le Mans 24-hour race. The original GT40s were constructed in England, at Slough, under the supervision of John Wyer, who had worked with previous Le Mans victors Aston Martin. Powered by a light alloy V8, the car was just 40 inches high – hence its name, Grand Touring 40. Three cars ran at Le Mans in 1964, one recording a speed of 187 mph, but all finally succumbed to mechanical failure. Development transferred to America, under the control of Carroll Shelby, who replaced the original V8 with a 427 cu. in. (7-liter) version. Six of these ran at Le Mans in 1965 but all suffered the same fate as their predecessors. Finally, after much further development work, GT40s took the first three places at Le Mans in 1966 and Ford decided to quit while it was ahead. A roadgoing variant of the MkII was produced in Slough and 31 examples were built. A "new" GT40 was marketed by Ford between 2004 and 2006.

| | |
|---|---|
| **Engine:** | Mid-mounted, V8 |
| **Capacity:** | 4736 cc |
| **Output:** | 306 bhp @ 6000 rpm |
| **Top Speed:** | 160 mph |
| **Acceleration:** | 0–60 in 5.3 seconds |

# FORD MUSTANG 1964

The Mustang – one of the most evocative model names in American motoring
history, ranking with Eldorado and Thunderbird – was born of necessity tempered
by invention. The American motor industry, along with the rest of US industry,
suffered from the decline in the American economy in the late fifties. As things
began to improve, manufacturers looked for a way to produce new models that
weren't too new, because that would be too expensive; a brave attempt to develop a
mid-engined Mustang roadster proved a little too brave. Under the inspired
guidance of Lee Iacocca, the original Mustang was produced almost entirely out of
stock parts and was based on an existing compact platform, that of the Falcon. The
car was scheduled to be launched at the New York World's Fair in April 1964 but
Walter Ford (Henry Ford II's nephew) "accidentally" took one out to a lunch date at
a restaurant in Detroit where a number of photographers just happened to be
waiting. Public reaction to the car was incredible; despite its humble origins it was
destined to become a star. Base models had a 100 hp six-cylinder engine, but most
buyers wanted a V8.

| | | | |
|---|---|---|---|
| **ENGINE:** | Front-mounted, V8 | **TOP SPEED:** | 118 mph |
| **CAPACITY:** | 289 cu. in. | **ACCELERATION:** | 0–60 in 9.0 seconds |
| **OUTPUT:** | 225 bhp @ 4800 rpm | | |

# FORD THUNDERBIRD 1955

"The Thunderbird is a new kind of sports car. We are convinced it will set a new trend in the automobile industry. It provides all of the comforts, conveniences and all-weather protection available in any of today's modern automobiles. It represents a successful combination of graceful, low-silhouette styling, spirited performance and outstanding roadability with dependable all-steel body construction." Thus spoke Ford's sales manager L. W. Smead at a press conference held at the Ford Styling Rotunda in 1954. He omitted to mention that Ford had hit upon the best name for a car in the history of motoring, conjuring as it does images of elemental power, grace, freedom and American heritage. He was concerned that everybody should understand that this was not a reaction to Chevrolet's Corvette. This was a new kind of sports car – i.e. not a sports car at all. It provided comforts and conveniences that the Corvette, with its pram hood and side-screens, lacked, and it had dependable all-steel body construction, whereas the Corvette was a fiberglass bath tub. He needn't have worried. With a name and looks like that, how could the Thunderbird fail? A "Retro-Bird" was produced in 2002.

| **ENGINE:** | Front-mounted, V8 | **TOP SPEED:** | 110 mph |
| **CAPACITY:** | 5113 cc | **ACCELERATION:** | 0–60 in 12.0 seconds |
| **OUTPUT:** | 225 bhp @ 4600 rpm | | |

# GORDON-KEEBLE GK1 1964

John Gordon ran a company called
Peerless Motors, based in Slough,
England. Jim Keeble ran a garage business
several hundred miles away in Ipswich.
One of Keeble's customers asked him to
fit a Chevrolet V8 into one of Gordon's
Peerless GTs, normally powered by a
rather more modest Triumph TR3 unit.
Both Gordon and Keeble felt that the
project had commercial promise and so
they went into partnership. Their
prototype, the Gordon GT, was shown at
the Geneva Motor Show in 1960. A
space-frame chassis was clothed with
bodywork styled by Giugiaro. A Corvette
V8 drove through a manual four-speed
transmission and a de Dion rear axle.
Production versions, now Gordon-Keeble
GK1s, replaced the original steel panels
with fiberglass. The overall result was a
very handsome 2+2 GT with all the finer
points of the E-Type Jaguar and the Aston
Martin DB4, plus a rustproof body that
both those cars would have benefited
from greatly. It was hugely civilized and
deceptively quick and, in a gesture of
pure, British understatement, its badge
was a tortoise. Sadly, buyers were not
prepared to pay so much for an unknown
quantity and only 99 were ever made.

| | |
|---|---|
| **ENGINE:** | Front-mounted, V8 |
| **CAPACITY:** | 5355 cc |
| **OUTPUT:** | 300 bhp @ 5000 rpm |
| **TOP SPEED:** | 137 mph |
| **ACCELERATION:** | 0–60 in 7.5 seconds |

# HONDA NSX 1990

The NSX was intended to demonstrate that Japan – or Honda, at least – could build a world-class sports car, and it did. Honda had long been pre-eminent in motorcycle sport and, in 1964, was the first Japanese manufacturer to take part in Formula One, so there was no shortage of competition experience to draw upon. Immense care was taken over the car's development, with numerous combinations of engine and running gear being tried and rejected. Eventually, a mid-engined coupé, styled by Pininfarina but managing not to look like an Italian look-alike, emerged, powered by a centrally located race-bred V6. Lightweight components were employed throughout and a sophisticated traction control system was fitted as standard. Many, especially Europeans, found the upstart from the East coarse, bland and flashy in about equal measures, but Americans, at whom the NSX was squarely aimed, valued the car, properly, for its fabulous performance and highly civilized road manners as well as for the sheer excitement that its superb screaming V6 engine could generate.

| | |
|---|---|
| **ENGINE:** | Mid-mounted, V6 |
| **CAPACITY:** | 2977 cc |
| **OUTPUT:** | 270p @ 7100 rpm |
| **TOP SPEED:** | 161 mph |
| **ACCELERATION:** | 0–60 in 5.9 seconds |

# HUDSON COMMODORE 1948

In the United States, as in Europe, most cars offered in the immediate post-war years were simply warmed-over pre-war models, but the Hudson was a magnificent exception to the rule. The new Hudson was based on a unibody (monocoque) design which, although not entirely new – Nash and Lincoln had already produced unibody designs – was innovative. Dispensing with chassis members allowed a significant lowering of the bodywork, producing what Hudson's advertising described as the "Step-Down" design: one stepped down into the car rather than climbing up into it. The car's roof line was lowered, adding to its rakish looks, and the result was a highly aerodynamic saloon with exceptionally nimble handling. Power was usually supplied by Hudson's simple but strong, Super Six engine which produced a mere 7 horsepower less than the alternative straight eight and was considerably lighter. Various transmission options were offered. The ultimate Step-Down Hudson was the Hornet, which achieved considerable success in NASCAR racing. Sadly, Hudson could never afford to develop a V8, and in the fifties Americans wanted V8s. Hudson disappeared in 1957.

| | |
|---|---|
| **ENGINE:** | Front-mounted, six cylinder |
| **CAPACITY:** | 262 cu. in. |
| **OUTPUT:** | 121 hp |
| **TOP SPEED:** | 115 mph |
| **ACCELERATION:** | 0–60 in 12.0 seconds |

# ISO GRIFO 1969

The Iso company of Milan was a
motorcycle manufacturing concern
which produced the Isetta bubble car
in the early 1950s. In 1955 it sold the
design to BMW and in 1960 came up
with a far more glamorous project.
The company's owner Renzo Rivolta
visited the Earls Court Motor Show
in London and was, understandably,
deeply impressed by the beautiful
Bertone-bodied, Corvette-powered,
Gordon-Keeble sports car displayed
there. He decided to repeat the
formula and produced the Bertone-
styled Iso Rivolta coupé in 1962. A
year later he turned again to Bertone
to produce a far more radically styled
two-seater, the Grifo. Engine capacity
and performance figures climbed
steadily and racing versions were
produced by Bizzarini, who marketed
the car in the United States as the
Bizzarini GT. In race tune these cars
could attain speeds in excess of 180
mph. Despite its bullet-proof
American power plant, the Grifo
proved too temperamental, even by
Italian standards, for most purchasers
and, sadly, far too rust-prone for all
but the most dedicated restorers.
Production ceased in 1974.
Resurrection has been threatened
but, as yet, has not materialized.

| | |
|---|---|
| **ENGINE:** | Front-mounted, V8 |
| **CAPACITY:** | 6998 cc |
| **OUTPUT:** | 390 bhp @ 5200 rpm |
| **TOP SPEED:** | 170 mph |
| **ACCELERATION:** | 0–60 in 7.1 seconds |

# ISO RIVOLTA 1962

The influence of the Gordon-Keeble is clearly seen in the elegant understated lines of the Iso Rivolta. This was the first car produced by Renzo Rivolta, owner of the Iso motorcycle factory in Milan. The chassis was designed and constructed by Giotto Bizzarini, who had worked extensively with Alfa Romeo and Ferrari. The 2+2 body styling, as with the Gordon-Keeble, was by Bertone. Engines and transmissions were imported from Detroit, again mimicking the GK1 by employing a Chevrolet V8. The Rivolta was intended to be a Grand Tourer rather than a sports car and so automatic transmission options, either Borg-Warner or GM Powerglide, were offered as well as a ZF manual five-speed gearbox. The Rivolta allowed rapid progress in considerable comfort and safety, for four, and the level of interior trim was of the highest quality. It may be that its sober styling failed to appeal to a mass market or that, as with the Gordon-Keeble, the "name" carried insufficient kudos. Production ceased in 1970.

| ENGINE: | Front-mounted, V8 |
|---|---|
| CAPACITY: | 5359 cc |
| OUTPUT: | 300 bhp @ 5000 rpm |
| TOP SPEED: | 125 mph |
| ACCELERATION: | 0–60 in 7.9 seconds |

# JAGUAR MKII 1960

A true sports saloon, the elegant and potent MkII Jaguar was the direct descendent of the MkI of 1956. The saloon's looks were greatly improved by the slimming down of the rear door pillars, giving the car an altogether more "airy" appearance. The beautifully balanced bodywork was the work of the great Sir William Lyons. The rear track was widened, though it remained narrower than the front and contributed to quite "exciting" cornering when the car was driven fast – and it could be driven very fast indeed, particularly when fitted with the 3.8-liter engine. Original engine options had been 2.4 liters (as on the MkI) and 3.4 liters. Wire wheels were a stylish and practical optional extra as they helped to cool the all-round disk brakes. The interior was sumptuous, generously trimmed in Connolly hide and a forest of walnut veneer. The MkII, like so many Jaguars, became immensely popular in America, where its combination of olde worlde charm and blistering performance was irresistible. In 1969 the down-graded 240 and 340 versions finally gave way to the XJ6, which had British Leyland written all over it.

| | | | |
|---|---|---|---|
| **ENGINE:** | Front-mounted, six cylinder | **TOP SPEED:** | 125 mph |
| **CAPACITY:** | 3781 cc | **ACCELERATION:** | 0–60 in 8.6 seconds |
| **OUTPUT:** | 220 bhp @ 5500 rpm | | |

# JAGUAR XJ220 1991

Originally intended to take the world by storm as the E-Type had done in the sixties, the XJ220 was the brainchild of Jaguar's chief engineer, Jim Randle. Power was to be supplied by a completely reworked version of the 5.3-liter V12, bored out to 6.2 liters and with twin overhead cams per cylinder bank with four valves per cylinder – which, some would say, is what it should have had in the first place. A massive effort went into producing a car for the Birmingham Motor Show in 1988, which featured bodywork styled by Keith Helfet that can only be described as fabulous. The car had upward-opening doors, four-wheel-drive, adaptive suspension and anti-lock brakes. Jaguar was acquired by Ford the following year; the project was coolly pursued. The "revised version" that appeared at the Tokyo Motor Show in 1991 had none of the above refinements, nor did it have a V12 engine. Power was now supplied by a Ford Cosworth-based 3.5-liter V6 with twin turbochargers. It was, until the advent of the McLaren F1, the fastest road car in the world, but not the car it should have been.

| | | | |
|---|---|---|---|
| **ENGINE:** | Mid-mounted, V6 | **TOP SPEED:** | 213 mph |
| **CAPACITY:** | 3498 cc | **ACCELERATION:** | 0–60 in 4.0 seconds |
| **OUTPUT:** | 542 bhp @ 7200 rpm | | |

# JAGUAR XK 2007

The latest Jaguar sports car, courtesy of the Ford Motor Company, looks as if it might just be the E-Type successor that Jag lovers have been waiting for – for three decades. A coupé was on sale in early 2006, to be followed, later in the year, by a convertible. Ian Callum's excellent, clean styling managed to retain a number of "signature" Jaguar features without stooping to "retro" detailing – this is a brand new, highly technologically advanced car and that's exactly what it looks like. The new XK features an all-aluminum monocoque structure. This adds stiffness and reduces weight at the same time. Power comes from Jaguar's well-tried V8 engine, but six-speed sequential automatic transmission is fitted, operated by paddles on either side of the wheel to allow "manual" shifts. An up-rated ABS braking system comes as standard, along with Bosch's Servotronic 2 electronic steering. Switchable TRAC Dynamic Stability Control with full traction control, plus a tire pressure monitor and run flat tires, no doubt makes the car as safe as it is exciting to drive.

| | |
|---|---|
| **ENGINE:** | Front-mounted, V8 |
| **CAPACITY:** | 4196 cc |
| **OUTPUT:** | 300 bhp @ 6000 rpm |
| **TOP SPEED:** | 155 mph |
| **ACCELERATION:** | 0–60 in 5.9 seconds |

# JAGUAR XK120 1948

The masterpiece of William Lyons (the Lyon behind every Jaguar) was unveiled at the 1948 London Motor Show. During the Second World War the company had developed a 3.4-liter six-cylinder engine with twin overhead camshafts – the legendary XK. This was intended to power a new luxury saloon, the MkVII, but found its way first into the sports car with the MkV chassis. The car's claimed performance was the subject of much heated debate and disbelief, but this was silenced by a specially prepared car attaining a speed of 132 mph on a stretch of Belgian motorway. Demand for this supremely elegant machine was massive, particularly from the United States, where it exerted enormous influence. The remarkable Harley Earl, GM's head of styling, himself drove an XK120. The lightweight aluminum paneling that graced the first examples was hastily replaced by steel for speed and simplicity in production. Fixed and drophead coupés followed, offering Jaguar's trademark leather and walnut interior luxury, but the nature of the beast was defined by its magnificent motor which would be retained, refined and developed until 1992.

| | |
|---|---|
| **ENGINE:** | Front-mounted, six cylinder |
| **CAPACITY:** | 3442 cc |
| **OUTPUT:** | 160 bhp @ 5000 rpm |
| **TOP SPEED:** | 120 mph |
| **ACCELERATION:** | 0–60 in 12.0 seconds |

# JAGUAR XKE E-TYPE 1961

The Jaguar E-Type is the definitive style icon of the swinging sixties in England. To those used to the dreary, lumbering saloons and rattling rev-boxes of the period, it appeared like a thing from another world. It seemed inconceivable that a car could be so sexy. That glorious styling was the work of Malcolm Sayer, who had previously produced Jaguar's superb sports-racing cars, the C-Type and the D-Type, but the E-Type was designed for the road and could be yours for £2000. Truly, we had never had it so good! First shown at Geneva, the car caused a sensation and it was capable, just, with a bit of tweaking, of 150 mph. Early examples featured a Moss gearbox that lacked synchromesh on first gear; this was the cause of the oft-heard "Ching!" as an E-Type pulled away. In 1966 a 4.2-liter version of the evergreen XK motor was fitted, improving low-end torque but giving no more speed. The headlight fairings were deleted; the cause, stated to be "upward light scatter," was probably cost. Various other incarnations followed, including a bulbous 2+2 and the overweight, 5.3-liter V12, which produced less power than the original (and best) 3.8.

| | |
|---|---|
| **Engine:** | Front-mounted, six cylinder |
| **Capacity:** | 3781 cc |
| **Output:** | 265 bhp @ 5500 rpm |
| **Top Speed:** | 150 mph |
| **Acceleration:** | 0–60 in 7.0 seconds |

# JAGUAR XKR 1998

First shown – like its illustrious predecessor the E-Type – at Geneva, the XKR was the quickest Jaguar ever, able to leap from rest to 60 mph in mere 5.2 seconds. The lusty supercharged V8 had twin cams per cylinder bank and was "blown" by an Eaton M112 unit. Drive was transmitted via an automatic five-speed gearbox. The XKR was available as either a coupé or a convertible but featured the XK8's rather bland "corporate" styling that relied far too heavily on the glories of the E-Type instead of establishing a strong identity of its own. A "limited edition" (special paint job) was produced in 2000 to mark Jaguar's entry into Formula One competition, and a "commemorative" version was offered in 2001 to mark the centenary of the birth of Jaguar's founder, Sir William Lyons. Even if Sir William might have been unimpressed by the XKR's styling, it is highly probable that he would have approved wholeheartedly of its performance. The XKR's top speed is governed to a modest 155 mph.

| ENGINE: | Front-mounted, V8 | TOP SPEED: | 155 mph |
|---|---|---|---|
| CAPACITY: | 3996 cc | ACCELERATION: | 0–60 in 5.2 seconds |
| OUTPUT: | 370 bhp @ 6150 rpm | | |

# JENSEN CV8 1962

In 1962, Jensen Motors of West Bromwich replaced the 4.5-liter Austin engine that had powered their fiberglass-bodied 541 models with American muscle: a Chrysler V8. The new car was, perhaps unimaginatively, named the CV8 and provided appropriately exclusive, luxurious, high-speed transport for the beautiful people of the swinging sixties. Unfortunately, a lot of those people didn't find the CV8 very beautiful. With its rather aggressive frowning "slant-eyed" headlights and a rear aspect that appeared to have been designed by a committee, the CV8 cannot be regarded as a contender for the most-beautiful-car-of-all-time prize. Furthermore, it was expensive to buy (a lot more expensive than a stylish E-Type Jaguar, for instance) and expensive to run, returning only 14 mpg. Nevertheless, the very rawness of the CV8's performance, even driving through Chrysler's indestructible Torqueflite three-speed automatic gearbox, won it many admirers and its rustproof shell has ensured the survival of a remarkable number of examples while later, steel-bodied Jensens have succumbed to corrosion.

| | | | |
|---|---|---|---|
| **ENGINE:** | Front-mounted, V8 | **TOP SPEED:** | 136 mph |
| **CAPACITY:** | 5910 cc | **ACCELERATION:** | 0–60 in 6.7 seconds |
| **OUTPUT:** | 330 bhp @ 4600 rpm | | |

# JENSEN FF 1966

The Jensen FF is a classic example of a
car that was truly ahead of its time.
Experiments had been carried out with
fitting a fully independent "Ferguson
Formula" four-wheel-drive system to the
CV8 but it was decided that Jensen had
to produce a car that was much more
appealing aesthetically as well as being
advanced technologically. The result was
the Interceptor FF. Styling was by Touring
of Milan but the original bodies were
manufactured by Vignale, before
production was transferred to West
Bromwich. The car looked sensational,
combining Italian flair with a bit of
British pugnacity. One of the most
striking features was the massive wrap-
around rear window, which allowed
excellent backward vision. Dunlop
"Maxaret" anti-lock brakes were fitted,
giving the car incredibly sure-footed
handling in almost any conditions. Sadly,
largely because of cost, customers
preferred the "cooking" version, *sans* FF
and Maxaret. An even more powerful
variant of the Interceptor, with a 7.2-liter
engine and triple carburetors – the SP –
followed in 1971, the year that the FF
option was deleted. The big engine, with
a single four-barrel carb, was used in all
Interceptor IIIs, including the rare coupé
and convertible.

| | |
|---|---|
| **Engine:** | Front-mounted, V8 |
| **Capacity:** | 6276 cc |
| **Output:** | 325 bhp @ 4690 rpm |
| **Top Speed:** | 130 mph |
| **Acceleration:** | 0–60 in 7.4 seconds |

# JENSEN-HEALEY 1974

The Jensen-Healey was a brave attempt to produce a traditional English sports car in the style of the MGB and the Triumph TR6. It was probably Jensen's intention that the car would extend the company's appeal into the increasingly important youth market. Donald Healey put together a very attractive package that pushed all the right buttons. It looked like a traditional sports car, it certainly went like a traditional sports car, but it also had about it a feeling of freshness and modernity that was unique. Power was supplied by a Lotus-developed twin-cam, all-alloy, four-cylinder engine, and in order to fit this under the J-H's low hood line, it was necessary to tip it over to one side. Servicing was tricky – this was a lot more complex than an MGB! Fluid gaskets on the cam covers were a weak point and the entire carburetor assembly (twin, twin-choke Dellortos) had to be removed in order to change the oil filter. The Jensen-Healey was a mechanical nightmare that drove like a dream. Series III cars were fitted with a five-speed gearbox and a closed, GT version was introduced at the bitter end. Jensen ceased production in 1976.

| | | | |
|---|---|---|---|
| **ENGINE:** | Front-mounted, four cylinder | **TOP SPEED:** | 125 mph |
| **CAPACITY:** | 1973 cc | **ACCELERATION:** | 0–60 in 7.0 seconds |
| **OUTPUT:** | 140 bhp @ 6500 rpm | | |

# LAGONDA 1976

Although the Lagonda of 1976 was, to all intents and purposes, a four-door Aston Martin V8, its individual identity was so strong that it deserves its own entry. David Brown purchased Aston Martin in 1947 and subsequently bought Lagonda to get hold of their splendid twin-cam six-cylinder engine, which powered the Aston Martins of the fifties. The Rapide, a saloon version badged as a Lagonda, was produced until 1964. An attempt to produce a new, four-door car in the early seventies foundered, but parts of the project were salvaged and employed in the 1976 car which was styled, sensationally, by William Towns. It is reported that Towns completed the design in a month. The car became the star of the 1976 London Motor Show. It wasn't just the striking – and extremely fashionable – wedge-shaped body that aroused such fascination, but the plethora of "space age" electronics. The dash panel appeared to be a blank piece of black glass until the car was started, whereupon it lit up with a futuristic graphic display – and spoke! The Lagonda contrived to look sporting and imposing at the same time. It was, and remains, without peer.

| | | | |
|---|---|---|---|
| **ENGINE:** | Front-mounted, V8 | **TOP SPEED:** | 141 mph |
| **CAPACITY:** | 5340 cc | **ACCELERATION:** | 0–60 in 8.8 seconds |
| **OUTPUT:** | 290 bhp | | |

# LAMBORGHINI COUNTACH 1974

"Countach!" is a Piedmontese expression implying surprise and admiration. The closest English approximation would maybe be just "Wow!" Looking at the car, it isn't difficult to understand why it drew this reaction from one of the factory workers on first seeing it. It is truly remarkable to think that the Countach was first shown to the public at the Geneva Motor Show in 1971. How many other thirty-five-year-old cars can still turn heads and draw a crowd? The engineering is as imaginative and daring as the styling – which was by Marcello Gandini of Bertone. The gearbox is placed ahead of the engine and the drive shaft actually passes through the sump. It took three years of development from the original unveiling to the first cars coming off the line. When they did, they required considerable skill and nerve to drive. The Countach predated traction control, reactive suspension and even anti-lock brakes. In the wet, it's a handful! Capacity was increased to 4.7 liters in 1982, and in 1985, to 5.2 liters, with the addition of four-valve heads which improved flexibility. There was an anniversary edition in 1988 to celebrate the car company's 25th birthday.

| | |
|---|---|
| **ENGINE:** | Mid-mounted, V12 |
| **CAPACITY:** | 3929 cc |
| **OUTPUT:** | 375 bhp @ 8000 rpm |
| **TOP SPEED:** | 175 mph |
| **ACCELERATION:** | 0–60 in 5.7 seconds |

# LAMBORGHINI ESPADA 1968

The Pirana was intended to carry Jaguar's much-vaunted V12 engine. Sadly, it didn't and we ended up with the XJS instead. Lamborghini was the beneficiary of British Leyland's timidity and mounted its own, rather more imaginative, V12 in Marcello Gandini's gorgeous Bertone body. The Espada is one of a very select group of automobiles that combine supercar performance with seating for four. It really is a very comfortable – even luxurious – motor, and it really does drive like a Lamborghini, provided one avoids the optional automatic transmission. Power-assisted steering, however – available on MkII cars – is a wise addition, as without it the Espada needs an awful lot of "driver input" at low speeds. The 2+2 Jarama coupé was introduced in 1970, but, despite its impressive performance, it looked rather lumpen against the Espada and its stablemate, the fabulous Miura. The Jarama was to be Lamborghini's last front-engined car.

| | | | |
|---|---|---|---|
| **ENGINE:** | Front-mounted, V12 | **TOP SPEED:** | 155 mph |
| **CAPACITY:** | 3929 cc | **ACCELERATION:** | 0–60 in 6.6 seconds |
| **OUTPUT:** | 350 bhp @ 7800 rpm | | |

# LAMBORGHINI GALLARDO 2003

The Gallardo is Lamborghini's new "entry level" offering, available in three versions:
the Gallardo 5.0, the Gallardo SE and the Gallardo Spider. The overall styling is
completely innovative but the Gallardo is still recognizably a "Lambo." The overall
impression is of muscularity and that's not misleading. Power is supplied by 90 degree
V10, based on the Audi 4.2-liter V8, developed by Cosworth. Eighty percent of the
engine's 520 Nm of torque is available at 1500 rpm. The entire aluminum space-frame
chassis weighs a mere 550 lb. The optional E-Gear transmission system offers three
settings: automatic, normal and sport. Automatic allows "easy" driving. Normal lets
the driver change gear manually, although when approaching peak revs, the electronics
will take over and shift upward automatically. The Sport setting will not change up
automatically but speeds up shift times dramatically. Koni's Frequency Selective
Damping allows a level of ride comfort previously unimaginable in a car such as this –
certainly in a Countach! The design and quality of the interior is commensurate with
the engineering. Everything about the Gallardo is superb.

| | | | |
|---|---|---|---|
| **ENGINE:** | Mid-mounted, V10 | **TOP SPEED:** | 195 mph |
| **CAPACITY:** | 4961 cc | **ACCELERATION:** | 0–60 in 4.2 seconds |
| **OUTPUT:** | 500 bhp @ 7800 rpm | | |

# LAMBORGHINI MIURA 1966

Lamborghini had only been in the car business for three years when they announced the Miura, which instantly became a household name that nobody could pronounce. The amazing styling was by Marcello Gandini of Bertone – and he was 26 at the time! The 3.5-liter quad-cam V12, designed by Giotto Bizzarini, was transplanted from Lamborghini's 350GT and the capacity increased to 3.9 liters. The engine was centrally located but, as with the Ford GT40, it was mounted transversely with the gearbox fitted below. One of the many striking details of the Miura was the "venetian blind" across the rear window, which serves a practical purpose in that it helps to dissipate engine heat. Similarly, the "eyelashes" that surround the rotating headlights are in fact louvered vents to assist in cooling the front brakes. The Miura was as much a sixties pinup as Brigitte Bardot, only marginally more attainable. Handling on early cars was not quite up to performance, however, as the Miura's nose exhibited an alarming tendency to lift at speed. Suspension and aerodynamics were gradually improved to eliminate the problem.

| | |
|---|---|
| **ENGINE:** | Mid-mounted, V12 |
| **CAPACITY:** | 3929 cc |
| **OUTPUT:** | 350 bhp @ 7000 rpm |
| **TOP SPEED:** | 171 mph |
| **ACCELERATION:** | 0–60 in 6.0 seconds |

# LAMBORGHINI MURCIELAGO 2001

The Murcielago is the first Lamborghini to be produced under VW ownership, development of the marque having been delegated to Audi. Lack of research and development funds had rendered Lamborghini unable to deliver a significant new model to replace the Diablo, which was itself a descendant of the 1971 Countach. Audi put a lot of time, talent and – most importantly – money into the project and its investment has paid off mightily. The Murcielago is visually striking while still managing to appear almost understated. A six-speed gearbox has replaced the Diablo's five-speed and, unsurprisingly given Audi's involvement, the car has permanent four-wheel drive. The simplicity of the body's line is retained by having a number of moving flaps and a spoiler, to aid engine cooling and improve high-speed stability respectively. The nose of the car can be raised almost 2 inches to allow it to pass over speed bumps. It seems that nothing has been left to chance. On top of all this, the Murcielago is widely regarded as the easiest Lamborghini to drive.

| | |
|---|---|
| **ENGINE:** | Mid-mounted, V12 |
| **CAPACITY:** | 6192 cc |
| **OUTPUT:** | 571 bhp @ 7500 rpm |
| **TOP SPEED:** | 205 mph |
| **ACCELERATION:** | 0–60 in 3.8 seconds |

# LANCIA AURELIA 1950

The Lancia Aurelia was the first car ever to be powered by a V6 engine. The design process had begun during the Second World War under the supervision of Francesco de Virgilio, a brilliant engineer, who addressed the problem of balance in such a motor and discovered that the optimum angle between the cylinder banks must be 60 degrees. Post-war prototypes for a new Aprilia, however, only allowed for a 45 degree angle, because of the narrowness of the engine compartment. After much fruitless testing, the Aprilia was abandoned in favor of de Virgilio's design. The result was the B20 Aurelia. It is worth noting that the technical director of the project was none other than the legendary Vittorio Jano, who had been responsible for Alfa Romeo's magnificent P2 and P3 racers. Jano took charge of the chassis design, which incorporated fully independent rear suspension, while de Virgilio concentrated on the engine. The resultant car, clothed in a variety of beautiful bodies, none more ravishing than the B24 Spider and convertible, became the first post-war Italian classic.

| | | | |
|---|---|---|---|
| **ENGINE:** | Front-mounted, V6 | **TOP SPEED:** | 108 mph |
| **CAPACITY:** | 2451 cc | **ACCELERATION:** | 0–60 in 12.5 seconds |
| **OUTPUT:** | 118 bhp @ 5000 rpm | | |

# LANCIA DELTA INTEGRALE 2002

The original "cooking" version of the Lancia Delta was powered by a transversely mounted, 2-liter twin-cam four-cylinder engine with two valves per cylinder. In 1986, Lancia's first "Group A" rally car appeared, based on the four-wheel-drive turbocharged Delta HF development. In association with Abarth, Lancia began the development of the Integrale. In order to achieve homologation for sporting purposes, it was necessary for Lancia to produce and sell 5000 cars. Even without a right-hand-drive option this was no problem, as the car proved immensely popular. In competition form, the Integrale dominated World Championship rallying for five years. Despite its rather "boxy" looks, the Integrale was a delight to drive, being light and nimble, powerful and responsive. Though trim, electrics and build quality were slightly suspect, nothing could detract from the sheer driving pleasure that these cars could provide. Four-valve versions followed, and works examples were tuned to produce almost double the output of road versions, indicating a design of immense strength. Lancia has produced some great cars, but none was greater than this.

| | | | |
|---|---|---|---|
| **ENGINE:** | Front-mounted, four cylinder | **TOP SPEED:** | 135 mph |
| **CAPACITY:** | 1995 cc | **ACCELERATION:** | 0–60 in 5.0 seconds |
| **OUTPUT:** | 185 bhp @ 5300 rpm | | |

# LANCIA STRATOS 1974

The Stratos was created to enable Lancia to dominate production car racing and, in particular, rallying. Lancia was part of the Fiat empire, as was Ferrari, and so the decision was made simply to transplant the 2.4-liter Dino engine into the new car. This was comparatively simple as the Ferrari engine was designed to be mid-mounted. A minimum of 400 "road" cars had to be produced within a year to ensure qualification. Though these cars were expensive, it was not difficult to find buyers as the performance, coupled with the splendidly purposeful Bertone styling, made for a magnificently "macho" package. As usual, the two-valve head was soon replaced by a four-valve version and performance increased even further. The Stratos proved untouchable in competition and achieved victory in most of the world's toughest rallies. It was essentially a race car adapted, not very convincingly, for road use. In traffic it was a fractious and intractable beast, but so suited was it to competition that Lancia continued to make competition works cars long after production had ceased.

| | |
|---|---|
| **ENGINE:** | Mid-mounted, V6 |
| **CAPACITY:** | 2418 cc |
| **OUTPUT:** | 190 bhp @ 7000 rpm |
| **TOP SPEED:** | 140 mph |
| **ACCELERATION:** | 0–60 in 5.4 seconds |

# LOTUS ELAN 1963

The new Lotus Elan was by far the most "civilized" car that Colin Chapman's company had produced, but happily it wasn't too civilized. The lightweight, fiberglass body was mounted on an extremely rigid "backbone" chassis, which gave the car fantastic handling characteristics. The 1.5-liter Lotus/Ford engine provided more than sufficient power to justify the car's name. The Elan performed with ... élan. The Porsche-style four-speed gearbox was extremely light in operation but very tough, encouraging enthusiastic driving – and the car was wonderfully cheeky, with its pop-up headlights that some owners adapted to give a "wink" at pedestrian crossings. Luggage capacity was pretty much "overnight" only and weather protection was minimal, but here was a genuine race car experience that could be had for a few thousand dollars. You could even build up your own from a kit! Though often described as a tourer, the Elan wasn't really at home on freeways and on a long journey the engine noise, coupled with hard suspension, could become very wearing. Given a stretch of country road, however, with plenty of twists and turns and changes of gradient and camber, it provided a level of sheer fun that was hard to match at any price.

| | |
|---|---|
| **ENGINE:** | Front-mounted, four cylinder |
| **CAPACITY:** | 1498 cc |
| **OUTPUT:** | 100 bhp @ 5700 rpm |
| **TOP SPEED:** | 110 mph |
| **ACCELERATION:** | 0–60 in 9.4 seconds |

# LOTUS ELISE 1995

The Lotus Elise might be described as the Elan for the new millennium. Like its illustrious forerunner, the Elise was intended to provide maximum driver satisfaction with a minimum of unnecessary extras – like comfort and practicality. This was intended to be a basic, no-frills sports car and it surely was. Constructed around a bonded aluminum chassis and tub with lightweight composite fiberglass bodywork, the Elise was spartan and purposeful. The major difference between the nineties Elise and the sixties Elan was the fact that the Elise's engine was mid-mounted, giving quite phenomenal road holding. Power was supplied by an aluminum Rover K series engine linked to a robust five-speed close ratio trans-axle gearbox – very close to the recipe used for the MGF. The Elise was possibly more appealing as a driver's car than the Elan had been, but unfortunately the world had moved on. There were few times and places where the Elise could demonstrate its excellent qualities to full effect, and for everyday motoring, its stripped-down simplicity seemed to verge on eccentricity. Good as it was, and is, the Elise became, effectively, a fashion accessory.

| | | | |
|---|---|---|---|
| **ENGINE:** | Mid-mounted, four cylinder | **TOP SPEED:** | 124 mph |
| **CAPACITY:** | 1796 cc | **ACCELERATION:** | 0–60 in 5.7 seconds |
| **OUTPUT:** | 118 bhp @ 5500 rpm | | |

# LOTUS ELITE 1957

Not to be confused with the seventies monstrosity that bore its name, the original
Lotus Elite was a classic British sports car. Colin Chapman had established his
company's reputation firmly on the track before producing his first car for the road;
the Elite was it and it was superb. Construction was revolutionary; the chassis was a
fiberglass monocoque reinforced with steel tubes. Were it not for the Corvette, the
Lotus Elite would be the world's first fiberglass-bodied car produced in significant
numbers. Powered by a small Coventry Climax engine with an overhead camshaft
that drove through a rugged four-speed gearbox, the Elite needed to be driven hard
and rewarded the driver that rose to the challenge. Great numbers of them were
raced, with great success. The Elite was a car that didn't mind being thrown around,
its fiberglass frame coping remarkably well. The body, designed by Peter Kirwan-
Taylor, was extremely sleek for a fifties car, and it is easy to see the inspiration for
the Elan, especially at the rear. Sadly, the cost of production meant that the Elite
didn't make much of a profit for Lotus, but it made a great impression.

| | | | |
|---|---|---|---|
| **ENGINE:** | Front-mounted, four cylinder | **TOP SPEED:** | 115 mph |
| **CAPACITY:** | 1216 cc | **ACCELERATION:** | 0–60 in 11.3 seconds |
| **OUTPUT:** | 83 bhp @ 6300 rpm | | |

# LOTUS ESPRIT 1976

Like the little girl in Longfellow's verse, the striking Giugiaro-styled Lotus Esprit could be very good indeed – but when she was bad, she was horrid. Eschewing spartan simplicity, Lotus embraced seventies style with a sleek wedge-shaped mid-engined luxuriously appointed pocket supercar. Following on from the less ostentatious Europa, it looked like a Ferrari, except it didn't have a V12 engine. Instead, the Esprit was powered by a twin-cam sixteen-valve aluminum four-pot, inclined at 45 degrees and displacing just over two liters. This engine had worked fine for the Jensen-Healey, a traditional, ragtop sports car, but it was hard pushed to deliver the goods that the Esprit's looks promised. Cooling was a major problem, and the front-mounted fans were notorious for sucking up road debris, sometimes with catastrophic results. Turbocharging increased output but put more stress on an already stressed power plant. On a good day, the Esprit could be a good car but, despite its elegant exterior, it was a bag of bits: bits of Citroën, bits of Opel, bits of Lancia – bits of everything. All in all, the pre-1987 Esprits were a bit of a disappointment. They got better.

| | |
|---|---|
| **Engine:** | Mid-mounted, four cylinder |
| **Capacity:** | 2174 cc |
| **Output:** | 210 bhp @ 6000 rpm |
| **Top Speed:** | 115 mph |
| **Acceleration:** | 0–60 in 11.3 seconds |

# LOTUS EUROPA 1966

The Europa was Lotus's first mid-engined road car. The company had plenty of experience of this layout – gained from racing – and applied it very imaginatively in this neat little hybrid. The engine and transmission were supplied by Renault and came from the 16. The Renault 16 was a front-wheel-drive car and so some modification was necessary, but it was achieved with total success. The plan was for the car to be marketed via Renault dealerships throughout Europe – hence the name. Lotus's by now well-tried backbone-chassis/fiberglass-body recipe was repeated, the body at first being bonded to the chassis, but later – for ease of maintenance and repair – bolted on. Handling was superb but the car felt underpowered. This was eventually remedied by the employment of a Ford twin-cam 1500, as in the Elan. The Europa caught the mood of the times well. It was stylish without being flashy; it had charm; it was groovy. Even though it didn't pretend to be anything but a two-seater, accommodation was still tight. Maybe it was the French influence, but the Europa seemed the perfect car for chic young lovers in the summer of love – and there's a new one.

| | |
|---|---|
| **ENGINE:** | Mid-mounted, four cylinder |
| **CAPACITY:** | 1470 cc |
| **OUTPUT:** | 78 bhp @ 6000 rpm |
| **TOP SPEED:** | 115 mph |
| **ACCELERATION:** | 0–60 in 7.5 seconds |

# LOTUS EXIGE 2000

The Exige is an extension of the Elise and, like its predecessor, seems to seek to extol the virtues of cold shower motoring in an age of the communal hot tub – but at least the Exige has a lid on it. The car bristles with race-bred technology. The extruded aluminum epoxy-bonded chassis is incredibly light and the fiberglass body is incredibly strong. The brakes are of aluminum composite material. Inspiration has obviously been drawn from the 200 bhp Elise Coupé, developed exclusively for racing and capable of 150 mph plus. The Exige is full of sound and fury and exudes character but it's all ever so slightly bogus. The stripped bare cockpit has mounting points for a full in-car entertainment outfit. Handling and road holding are beyond reproach but performance, given the huge spoiler on the outside and the racing harness on the inside, is no better than many executive saloons. Dare one suggest that it's a bit of a sheep in wolf's clothing?

| | |
|---|---|
| **ENGINE:** | Mid-mounted, four cylinder |
| **CAPACITY:** | 1796 cc |
| **OUTPUT:** | 190 bhp @ 7800 rpm |
| **TOP SPEED:** | 124 mph |
| **ACCELERATION:** | 0–60 in 5.5 seconds |

# LYNX XKSS 1957/2007

Jaguar built sixteen XKSSs, converted for road use from leftover D-Types when the company withdrew from racing in 1956. Lynx, a firm specializing in the precise recreation of classic Jaguars for discerning and extremely wealthy individuals, has, to date, built ten. Lynx is based in East Sussex, England. The Company was founded in 1968, by engineer Guy Black and architect Roger Ludgate. They produced their first new/old car – the Lynx D-Type – in 1974. Such is the quality of their work that they managed to weather the storms of the boom-and-bust eighties and continue to flourish in a niche market entirely of their own creation. Panels are hand-formed in aluminum over a wooden "buck." Engines, usually acquired – like donated organs – from deceased E-Types, are stripped down and rebuilt with infinite care. The result is a masterpiece – or is it a fake? The original XKSS was rough and ready and rudimentary, with a monocoque chassis and a tubular front subframe. It employed a highly tuned version of the Jaguar XK six-cylinder twin-cam engine, fitted with triple Weber carburetors. It was extremely rare and extremely desirable – and so is the Lynx.

| | |
|---|---|
| **ENGINE:** | Front-mounted, six cylinder |
| **CAPACITY:** | 3442 cc |
| **OUTPUT:** | 250 bhp @ 6000 rpm |
| **TOP SPEED:** | 145 mph |
| **ACCELERATION:** | 0–60 in 5.2 seconds |

# MASERATI 3500GT 1957

The beauty of the Maserati 3500GT, as with so many Italian exotics of the period, lay in the wide variety of beautiful bodies that could be created to clothe the car and the magnificent engine that lay at the heart of it. In the case of the 3500GT, coachwork was produced by Touring and Vignale, and the rare 5000GT had Allemano bodywork. The 3500GT was powered by Maserati's super, race-bred twin-cam six-cylinder unit. Other parts were simply bought in: a German ZF gearbox; a British Salisbury back axle, and so on. The result was a very fine high-speed tourer that would become the basis for a long and successful line of Maserati coupés and Spiders. It was followed by the 3500GTi, with Lucas fuel injection; the Vignale-bodied Sebring and the Mistral, with coachwork by Frua. Over 3500 cars were built over a 12-year period, every one of them elegant, potent and desirable. The 3500GT, with its race-proven engine and "rugged" suspension layout, proved a tempting option when compared to some of the hugely temperamental machines being produced by some other Italian manufacturers at the time.

| **ENGINE:** | Front-mounted, six cylinder | **TOP SPEED:** | 130 mph |
| **CAPACITY:** | 3485 cc | **ACCELERATION:** | 0–60 in 8.1 seconds |
| **OUTPUT:** | 235 bhp @ 5550 rpm | | |

# MASERATI BORA 1972

The Bora was Maserati's first mid-engined road car and combined tremendous performance with superb road-holding and a very high level of refinement. This was a very sophisticated Grand Tourer indeed, and Maserati's answer to the challenge issued by Lamborghini in the sublime shape of the Miura. Suddenly, front-engined supercars weren't super anymore, not even the glorious Ferrari Daytona. Maserati had considerable experience with mid-engined designs, gained largely from its remarkable 'bird cage" sports racers, but it knew little about unitary construction. It says much for Giulio Alfieri, Maserati's chief engineer, that the problems inherent in the mid-engined layout were overcome with such efficiency and panache. The admirably unfussy styling was by Ital Design. The car looked chunky and purposeful without any hint of macho self-consciousness. The interior was amazingly airy and roomy for a mid-engined car, and it was comfortable – and it was quiet! Citroën hydraulics were utilized extensively, resulting in slightly on–off braking, a characteristic inherited by the Bora's charming little sister, the Merak. The Bora's prodigious thirst, especially at the time of the seventies oil crisis, coupled with the parting of Citroën and Maserati, restricted the Bora's production run to fewer than 600.

| | | | |
|---|---|---|---|
| **ENGINE:** | Mid-mounted, V8 | **TOP SPEED:** | 162 mph |
| **CAPACITY:** | 4719 cc | **ACCELERATION:** | 0–60 in 6.5 seconds |
| **OUTPUT:** | 310 bhp @ 6000 rpm | | |

# MASERATI GHIBLI 1996

The defining quality of the Ghibli is refinement. The original design was distilled from years of experience gained on both road and track by the incomparable Giulio Alfieri, Maserati's technical director. The engine was reliable and the styling, by Giugiaro, was restrained. This was a car for people of taste; it was a car that whispered rather than screamed. In many ways, the layout of the Ghibli: front engine, rear drive, rigid back axle, was rather basic, but there was no doubting its effectiveness. By any standards, the Ghibli was quick and sure-footed. Taking into account that the Ghibli weighed over a ton and half, these characteristics seem all the more impressive. Here was a car that drivers and passengers alike could savor over the longest drive: elegant, effortless progress. The Ghibli appeared to represent the end of an era in supercar design, but Maserati has returned to the theme and improved what seemed unimprovable. In 1995, the one marque, Ghibli Open Cup racing series was initiated and a special commemorative model introduced. It is reported that every car completed the 9 race series without needing an engine rebuild – a great encouragement for road drivers.

| | |
|---|---|
| **ENGINE:** | Front-mounted, V6 |
| **CAPACITY:** | 1990 cc |
| **OUTPUT:** | 330 bhp @ 7000 rpm |
| **TOP SPEED:** | 165 mph |
| **ACCELERATION:** | 0–60 in 5.5 seconds |

# MASERATI MC12 2006

"Maserati has designed a new road-going Grand Tourer known as the MC12 from which a GT racing version has also been developed. The result is that 37 long years after its last victory in an international championship (1967, Cooper Maserati F1, South African Grand Prix), the Trident is returning to the track." Thus spoke Maserati's press office, to the amazement of many. The MC12 represents a complete change of direction for Maserati, comparable to the introduction of its first mid-engined car, the Bora, in 1972. The MC12 – one hopes that it will be given a proper name – will be available to private customers in blue and white livery only, harking back to the great days of Stirling Moss and the Tipo 60–61 "Birdcage" sports racers, so called because of their space-frame chassis design. The MC12's chassis is formed from a carbon-fiber and Nomex honeycomb sandwich. Nomex is a flame-retardant fiber developed by DuPont. The MC12 features a removable hard top and a cabin filled with the latest technology and yet is still redolent of Maserati's luxury GTs. The six-speed, computerized gearbox is operated by paddles and has but two modes: sport and racing.

| | |
|---|---|
| **ENGINE:** | Mid-mounted, V12 |
| **CAPACITY:** | 5998 cc |
| **OUTPUT:** | 630 bhp @ 7500 rpm |
| **TOP SPEED:** | 210 mph |
| **ACCELERATION:** | 0–60 in 3.7 seconds |

# MASERATI QUATTRO-PORTE 2005

Maserati Quattroportes have been around for many years and have always represented the ultimate in high-performance luxury motoring. The latest offering is no exception; in fact it's the best yet. Elegantly styled by Pininfarina, the 16-foot-long Quattroporte has near-perfect weight distribution and handles like a sports car. The electronic six-speed sequential gearbox, operated – as is becoming standard practice – via fingertip controlled paddles, allows for maximum fun with minimum fuss on the highway and yet the car is tractable and docile in city driving conditions. The interior is sumptuous but, as always with Maseratis, supremely tasteful: there's nothing flashy about this car; it does everything asked of it with poise and panache, and unique style. Limousine comfort is combined, seamlessly, with competition performance; one cannot ask for much more. Certain German and British manufacturers will have to look to their laurels to match the Maserati's "grace, space and pace" – as Jaguar advertisements used to say.

| | |
|---|---|
| **ENGINE:** | Front-mounted, V8 |
| **CAPACITY:** | 4244 cc |
| **OUTPUT:** | 400 bhp @ 7000 rpm |
| **TOP SPEED:** | 175 mph |
| **ACCELERATION:** | 0–60 in 5.2 seconds |

# MAZDA RX-7 1978

Over half a million RX-7s were produced between 1978 and 1985 – a testament to the efficiency and effectiveness of the Wankel rotary engine, over which Mazda had kept its nerve when all around were losing interest. The advantages of the design are fewer moving parts and extremely smooth power delivery. The drawbacks, initially, were high fuel and oil consumption and the seemingly insurmountable difficulty of providing seals for the rotor apexes that would withstand the stresses exerted on them. Buyers of NSU's ground-breaking Ro80 were unable to resist exploiting the turbine-like power delivery of the motor, resulting in regular – and expensive – blowing of the seals. Mazda's neat coupé, with its impressively aerodynamic styling, gained an army of converts. The car drove like a European GT, with a (rather notchy) five-speed gearbox and excellent, predictable handling. Owners were encouraged to curb the enthusiasm that the engine engendered by the fitting of a buzzer, which sounded when revs exceeded 6000. The steering was heavy at low speeds, but on the open road the Mazda shone. A turbocharged version was introduced in 1985 and the line continues to this day in the shape of the splendid RX-8.

| | |
|---|---|
| **Engine:** | Front-mounted, twin rotor Wankel |
| **Capacity:** | 2292 cc |
| **Output:** | 100 bhp @ 6000 rpm |
| **Top Speed:** | 125 mph |
| **Acceleration:** | 0–60 in 8.9 seconds |

# McLAREN F1 1993

The McLaren F1 has retained its crown as the world's fastest production car for over a decade, but in order to maintain even a slender margin of superiority over its rivals, the cost of building – and buying – it was astronomic. Unveiled on the eve of the 1993 Monaco Grand Prix (won by a McLaren, happily) the car carried a price tag that was uncomfortably close to $1million. What prospective purchasers got for their money was a car that had been designed, from the ground up, by a winning Formula One team. Built around a "tub" exactly like an F1 car, the McLaren was powered by a 6-liter quad-cam BMW V12 via a six-speed gearbox, with a stick shift. The F1 could seat three abreast, with the driver between and slightly ahead of the passengers. Performance was, not surprisingly, incredible, as was safety. It was not uncommon to see these cars trundling over the Hog's Back, a well-known ridge close to Woking, Surrey, where they were built. One wonders if they were ever "opened up" and what the reaction of the local constabulary might have been; pursuit would have been pointless. Production ceased in 1997.

| | |
|---|---|
| **ENGINE:** | Mid-mounted, V12 |
| **CAPACITY:** | 6064 cc |
| **OUTPUT:** | 627 bhp @ 7400 rpm |
| **TOP SPEED:** | 240 mph |
| **ACCELERATION:** | 0–60 in 3.2 seconds |

# MERCEDES 230SL 1963

The Mercedes 230SL incorporated all that is best in German design and engineering. It had crisp styling; it was beautifully built; it performed efficiently; and it was totally reliable. It also had a degree of charm and style that German cars often lack. The 230SL was a fun car without being frivolous. Unveiled at the Geneva Motor Show in 1963, the car was powered by a lusty fuel-injected six-cylinder engine that provided plenty of smoothly delivered power. A four-speed manual gearbox came as standard but automatic transmission was available as an option. All-independent suspension, coupled with a wide track, provided an exceptionally stable ride and confident handling. This smart roadster could be transformed into a luxury GT simply by fitting the substantial hardtop. This was slightly dished and became known as the "pagoda" roof. In either configuration, the car looked extremely smart. Engine capacity was gradually increased, giving more rapid acceleration but not much additional top speed. Despite its high price tag, the 230SL's sheer quality made it a best-seller.

| | | | |
|---|---|---|---|
| **ENGINE:** | Front-mounted, six cylinder | **TOP SPEED:** | 124 mph |
| **CAPACITY:** | 2281 cc | **ACCELERATION:** | 0–60 in 10.3 seconds |
| **OUTPUT:** | 170 bhp @ 5600 rpm | | |

# MERCEDES 300SL 1954

Like the Lamborghini Countach, the Mercedes 300SL's best-known feature was its doors. These opened vertically and, when both were raised, looked like a gull's wings – hence the "Gullwing" Mercedes. The reason for this peculiarity was nothing to do with style, it was a matter of necessity. The 300SL was built on an extremely light, extremely rigid space-frame that consisted of a complex latticework of metal tubes – just as in the legendary "Birdcage" Maserati sports racers. There could be no gap in the framework and a conventional door would have been too small to allow entry or egress with any dignity, so the doors had to open upward. Even then, the steering wheel was designed to swing out of the way in order to allow the driver to get in and out. Because of this method of construction, the car was extremely light. It was also powerful, employing a massively robust, 3-liter single-cam six-cylinder engine that had already achieved success in competition. 300SLs scored memorable victories in Grand Prix racing, road racing and at Le Mans. In its day the 300SL was just about the fastest car on the road, with only Ferrari as a serious challenger.

| **Engine:** | Front-mounted, six cylinder | **Top Speed:** | 154 mph |
| **Capacity:** | 2996 cc | **Acceleration:** | 0–60 in 8.3 seconds |
| **Output:** | 190 bhp @ 6000 rpm | | |

# MERCEDES McLAREN SLR 2005

The Mercedes McLaren attempts to mix tradition with innovation, looking backward and forward at the same time. The result, inevitably, is a collision of cultures. The car results from the association of McLaren and Mercedes in Formula One racing and the MM is packed with competition-bred features. The body is made from carbon-fiber and aluminum, bonded to a structural "tub" exactly as in an F1 car. The twin superchargers scream like banshees as the throttle is opened; the exhausts bellow in sympathy; the whole experience has an oddly "vintage" feel. This is added to by the fact that one is sitting behind the engine, looking down a long hood, like driving a 300SL. And guess what; the McLaren has gullwing doors, for no reason at all other than that they are a Mercedes signature feature. Transmission is via a five-speed "manumatic" gearbox featuring the customary paddle shifters. Though road holding is beyond reproach, the suspension is unyielding. The whole feel of the car is rather raw, which may well appeal to many potential purchasers.

| | |
|---|---|
| **ENGINE:** | Front-mounted, V12 |
| **CAPACITY:** | 5496 cc |
| **OUTPUT:** | 617 bhp @ 6700 rpm |
| **TOP SPEED:** | 204 mph |
| **ACCELERATION:** | 0–60 in 3.8 seconds |

# MG A 1955

Three years after the MG company became part of the ill-starred British Motor
Corporation, the MG A, designed by Syd Enever, was unveiled to the world. It might
have arrived earlier had not BMC's chairman, Leonard Lord, given preference to the
Healey 100 as the Corporation's flagship sports model. Despite the delay, the MG A
went on to become the world's most popular sports car. Over 100,000 examples were
sold by the time the model was replaced – by the even more popular MG B – in 1962.
The MG A's popularity stemmed from a combination of factors. It was stylish, as a
sports car should be: a very modern-looking machine after the "T" series. It performed
well; it was robust, reliable and – most importantly – it was affordable. The vast majority
of MG As went to America, where they must have provided welcome relief from
Detroit's staid and stodgy sedans. A bubble-topped coupé became available and smart
wire wheels could be had at additional cost. Weather protection was still crude, however,
with clip-on side-screens instead of roll-up windows. The "twin cam" version offered
more performance but at the cost of reliability – it was a notorious piston burner.

| | | | |
|---|---|---|---|
| **ENGINE:** | Front-mounted, four cylinder | **TOP SPEED:** | 95 mph |
| **CAPACITY:** | 1488 cc | **ACCELERATION:** | 0–60 in 15.4 seconds |
| **OUTPUT:** | 72 bhp @ 5500 rpm | | |

# MG B 1962

As with the A, so with the B. The MG B was designed by Syd Enever, had an Austin engine and became the world's most popular sports car. As with the A, the vast majority went to the United States. The MG B was a more modern car than the MG A, just as that had been more modern than the T series MGs. The MG B was sophisticated and sexy and in tune with the sixties: it was youthful and fun and affordable. Wind-up windows were a welcome new feature, making winter driving much more comfortable The new body was of unitary construction and styled by Don Hayter. The GT version, introduced in 1965, was a massive success as it combined sportiness with practicality and, along with the Pininfarina-bodied Austin A40, was one of Britain's first "hatchbacks." A 3-liter version, the MG C, arrived in 1967 but never caught owing to its questionable handling characteristics, and the V8 incarnation of 1973, which borrowed Rover's borrowed Buick motor, was stillborn because of the oil crisis. The limited edition RV8 of 1992 was a fitting tribute to a much-loved car.

| | | | |
|---|---|---|---|
| **ENGINE:** | Front-mounted, four cylinder | **TOP SPEED:** | 102 mph |
| **CAPACITY:** | 1798 cc | **ACCELERATION:** | 0–60 in 12.0 seconds |
| **OUTPUT:** | 95 bhp @ 5400 rpm | | |

# MG TC 1945

The TC was the direct descendant of
the TA Midget, which so many
American servicemen had fallen in
love with when stationed in England
during the war. That car's spartan
image, with its folding screen and
rock-solid suspension, was immensely
appealing. The TC used exactly the
same formula: it was cheap to buy,
fun to drive and simple to maintain.
Most were exported, but not "across
the pond"; they went out instead to
what remained of the British Empire.
Sufficient numbers made their way to
the United States, however, to whet
America's appetite, which was finally
satisfied by the arrival of the TD. By
today's standards, the T series MGs
were hardly sports cars – any small
car could drag one off the lights and
leave it behind on the highway, but
with the hood down and the screen
folded, these cars were enormous fun
and many racing drivers began their
careers in them. The last of the line
was the elegant but hefty TF. The TD
is probably the best of the bunch, but
they're all as British as roast beef and
bitter beer.

| | |
|---|---|
| **ENGINE:** | Front-mounted, four cylinder |
| **CAPACITY:** | 1250 cc |
| **OUTPUT:** | 54 bhp @ 5200 rpm |
| **TOP SPEED:** | 78 mph |
| **ACCELERATION:** | 0–60 in 22.0 seconds |

# MG TF 1995

Enthusiasts across the globe were thrilled by the announcement of a new MG sports car, albeit with an old name. While under BMW control, the MG division had languished, but when the MG Rover group gained independence, the future seemed rosy. The MG sports car is a British icon. As with popular music, one can date oneself by MG period, at least until the seventies. MG was one of the items of "family silver" that was sold off, but what is heartbreaking is the state in which it was returned. A brief internet search is all that is necessary to discover the level of rage and frustration felt by those who have, in good faith, and sometimes in a spirit of patriotism, bought these cars. For the record, however, the MG TF is a two-seat roadster, powered by a rear-mounted twin-cam, four-cylinder engine. In the words of the official website, the TF retains the "real world" affordability and practicality that set the MG F apart from rival cars, but is even more faithful to the MG brand ethos of "Outrageous Fun For All." I think not. A hundred years of production at the Longbridge factory ended in April 2005.

| | |
|---|---|
| **ENGINE:** | Rear-mounted, four cylinder |
| **CAPACITY:** | 1588 cc |
| **OUTPUT:** | 116 bhp @ 6250 rpm |
| **TOP SPEED:** | 118 mph |
| **ACCELERATION:** | 0–60 in 9.2 seconds |

# MINI
# COOPER S 1964

The Cooper S was the competition
derivative of Alec Issigonis's mini-
masterpiece. The design of the Mini was
so innovative it was almost unbelievable,
particularly to a buying public accustomed
to such dreary old dons as the Morris
Oxford and the Austin Cambridge. This
tiny car had room for four people! This
was due to the transverse mounting of the
848 cc engine, which drove the front
wheels and thus dispensed with the need
for a transmission tunnel. The road
holding of the little front-wheel-drive car
was a revelation – it was nippy, it was
safe, it was cheap and, because of its
novelty, classless. The Mini rapidly became
as potent a symbol of swinging London as
the E-Type. John Cooper recognized the
car's competition potential and suggested
a "hotter" variant, powered by a 55 bhp,
twin-carb version of the Leyland A series
engine. The power plant was gradually
enlarged until, in 1964, the definitive
example emerged with up-rated
suspension. A Mini Cooper driven by
Paddy Hopkirk won the Monte Carlo rally
that year and further victories followed –
some of them disputed. The BMW Mini
of 2001 also has a Cooper variant –
imitation being the sincerest form of
flattery.

| | |
|---|---|
| **ENGINE:** | Front-mounted, four cylinder |
| **CAPACITY:** | 1275 cc |
| **OUTPUT:** | 76 bhp @ 5800 rpm |
| **TOP SPEED:** | 98 mph |
| **ACCELERATION:** | 0-60 in 10.9 seconds |

# MONTEVERDI 375S 1969

Peter Monteverdi was a Ferrari dealer, based in Geneva. During the late sixties and early seventies, he set up a small works to produce the ultimate luxury car, mating American power to Italian design. Monteverdi subscribed to the view that there is no substitute for cubes and so equipped his cars with Mopar's most massive offerings: Chrysler hemis displacing up to 440 cu.in. – 7.5 liters. It is rumored that part of his motivation, as with Lamborghini, was frustration with Enzo Ferrari's legendary indifference to customer input. Monteverdi produced a series of exquisitely beautiful GT coupés, styled by Frua, that would easily bear comparison with any others. The cars had a rectangular section space-frame chassis and much of the running gear, bar the Chrysler Torqueflite transmission, came from Jaguar. Drivers report that performance is comparable to other American-powered Europeans of the period such as the Jensen Interceptor or the Bristol 911, the Facel Vega or the Gordon-Keeble, but the Monteverdi was more beautiful than any of them. Few were ever built, they have languished for years, but values are finally, and rightly, rising.

| | |
|---|---|
| **Engine:** | Front-mounted, V8 |
| **Capacity:** | 440 cu. in. |
| **Output:** | 375 hp |
| **Top Speed:** | 150 mph |
| **Acceleration:** | 0–60 in 6.3 seconds |

# MORGAN AERO 8 2000

Morgan motors has been in existence since 1910. This tiny company, based amidst some of the finest scenery in England, at Malvern Link in Worcestershire, has survived two world wars, tax changes, fashion changes, recession, oil crises and constant competition. Morgan must be doing something right. For as long as anyone cares to remember, Morgan have had full order books for their 1930s-style sports cars. The Plus 4 and the Plus 8, in various forms, have kept buyers waiting for a decade for decades. Now they've come up with something new – it's the same, only different. In time-honored fashion, the Aero's aluminum monocoque body is mated to an ash frame. Power comes from a BMW V8, as used in 5 Series saloons, specially prepared to Morgan's specifications and driving through a six-speed, Getrag gearbox. The bodywork manages to be retro and futuristic at the same time and will divide many as to its attractiveness. What is remarkable is that the Aero has an extremely low drag coefficient of 0.39 and this, combined with the car's light weight, allows for shattering performance.

| | |
|---|---|
| **Engine:** | Front-mounted, V8 |
| **Capacity:** | 4398 cc |
| **Output:** | 286 bhp @ 5500 rpm |
| **Top Speed:** | 160 mph |
| **Acceleration:** | 0–60 in 4.7 seconds |

# MORGAN PLUS 4 2006

Between 1910 and 1950, Morgan built three-wheelers and was unchallenged in the field. It may be that it was this early experience of niche-marketing that has enabled Morgan to continue – some might say persist – in making 1930s cars when everyone else stopped in the 1940s. Their first four-seater, four-wheeler, the 4/4, was marketed in 1935, using a Coventry Climax engine, and was revived after the war, powered by a Standard Vanguard unit. The 4/4 has continued in production, using a variety of power plants, until the present day – that's 70 years. The two-seater Plus 4 was introduced in 1950 and has continued to be manufactured using a number of engines over the years – one of the most memorable being the Triumph TR unit in the sixties. The latest car employs a Rover-derived, sixteen-valve, light alloy four-cylinder power plant that gives very spirited performance. Despite its quaint appearance, the Morgan complies with all current safety and emission regulations and thus provides a vintage motoring experience without the headaches of a vintage car.

| | | | |
|---|---|---|---|
| **ENGINE:** | Front-mounted, four cylinder | **TOP SPEED:** | 120 mph |
| **CAPACITY:** | 1999 cc | **ACCELERATION:** | 0–60 in 7.5 seconds |
| **OUTPUT:** | 145 bhp @ 6000 rpm | | |

# MORGAN PLUS 8 1968

The Plus 8, powered by the ever-popular all-aluminum Buick-derived, Rover 3.5-liter V8 engine, was first produced in 1968. It continues to fill Morgan's order books and the waiting list is very, very long. The Plus 4 had been employing the 2.2-liter engine from the Triumph TR4 – and very well it suited the Morgan too – but the demise of the TR4a in 1967, and the announcement that Triumph were moving to a six-cylinder engine for the TR5, gave Morgan a problem – the new Triumph engine wouldn't fit. By happy chance, the Rover/Buick V8 would, with a bit of shoe-horning, and thus the Plus 8 was born. The wheelbase had to be lengthened slightly and the track was widened to help with roadholding when all that extra power was applied. The rest was just as before, right down to the non-synchro Moss gearbox! This was replaced by a Rover five-speed unit in 1976. Fuel injection followed in 1984, and in 1990 capacity was increased to 4 liters plus – there was an optional 4.6-liter version. Bodies were formed entirely of aluminum, but mounted, as ever, to a hand-formed, ash frame.

| | | | |
|---|---|---|---|
| **ENGINE:** | Front-mounted, V8 | **TOP SPEED:** | 125 mph |
| **CAPACITY:** | 3529 cc | **ACCELERATION:** | 0–60 in 6.8 seconds |
| **OUTPUT:** | 160 bhp @ 5200 rpm | | |

# NOBLE M12 GTO 2000

The GTO label might be a bit cheeky, but nevertheless the Noble M12 is a tremendous car — the sort of car that Lotus should surely be building by now. Good luck to Lee Noble and his little company in Cosby, Leicestershire, England: his is a brave — dare one say, noble — endeavor. The chassis is a steel space-frame with bonded alloy panels, incorporating a full roll-cage. The body is made from a GRP composite with detachable front and rear sections. There's a choice of engines: a 1.8-liter four-cylinder Ford Zetec or a Ford V6 with twin Garrett turbochargers. The car is phenomenally capable in either form and each one is completed to the customer's personal specification. The ride is very firm, obviously, but not rough; the Noble is raw but it isn't ragged. The interior is exemplary: it's simple and functional — and comfortable — and it all comes together properly, as if it's been designed beforehand rather than thrown together as an afterthought. Full racing harness is supplied and justified. The 1.8 M12 is worth considering by anyone contemplating buying an Exige; the 2.5 M12 is worth considering by anyone contemplating buying a Veyron.

| | |
|---|---|
| **ENGINE:** | Mid-mounted, V6 |
| **CAPACITY:** | 2595 cc |
| **OUTPUT:** | 310 bhp @ 6000 rpm |
| **TOP SPEED:** | 155 mph |
| **ACCELERATION:** | 0–60 in 3.9 seconds |

# NSU RO80 1967

This was, in fact, a revolutionary car. Maybe it's something to do with the inventor's name, but Felix Wankel's rotary engine has never really caught on. The only producer to have persevered is Mazda and its faith has been rewarded – the RX8 sells. The Ro80 was an ambitious project for 1967, even without the Wankel engine. The car was a full-size saloon with very sculptured lines. It featured front-wheel drive, with a semi-automatic gearbox, rack and pinion steering and inboard disk brakes at the front – more nineties spec than sixties. The engine was a twin-rotor Wankel unit, displacing the equivalent of about 2 liters. Oil had to be mixed with the petrol to lubricate the "cylinders," creating major emission problems, and the cast-iron seals on the tips of the triangular rotors were badly prone to failure. Buyers were, understandably, wary. About 40,000 were built and it was the last NSU ever. NSU, incidentally, is derived from the names of the two rivers that flowed past the original factory: the *N*eckar and the *S*ulm.

| | |
|---|---|
| **ENGINE:** | Front-mounted, twin-rotor Wankel |
| **CAPACITY:** | 1990 cc |
| **OUTPUT:** | 115 bhp @ 5500 rpm |
| **TOP SPEED:** | 106 mph |
| **ACCELERATION:** | 0–60 in 14.2 seconds |

# PAGANI ZONDA C12 1999

Horacio Pagani named his amazing car out of respect and affection for Juan Manuel Fangio, a fellow Argentinean widely regarded as the greatest racing driver of all time. Such is the reverence that Pagani feels for his hero that he refrains from actually using his name, but remembers him as the Zonda – the wind from the Andes. From the original C12 to its latest incarnation, the Zonda has exemplified perfection in design, development and engineering. The cars are produced by Modena Design and the company has worked in close collaboration with both Ferrari and Lamborghini. Powered by Mercedes Benz AMG V12s, the car is constructed around a central carbon "tub" – a safety cell – which offers the occupants maximum security. The suspension system is crafted from aluminum and the bodywork is carbon fiber. There is no compromise in the Zonda's design. This is a car built for speed, but the driving experience seems at first to be uncannily relaxed. Noise levels are remarkably low and the ride is vibration-free. Six-speed transmission renders the car totally tractable at low speeds, but once the throttle is opened wide, the hidden nature of the beast is revealed.

| | |
|---|---|
| **Engine:** | Mid-mounted, V12 |
| **Capacity:** | 5987 cc |
| **Output:** | 394 bhp @ 5200 rpm |
| **Top Speed:** | 200 mph |
| **Acceleration:** | 0–60 in 4.2 seconds |

# PANTHER J72 1972

The Panther J72 was inspired by the SS Jaguar of 1935. Early models were powered by a 3.8-liter Jaguar XK engine, to be followed by 4.2s and V12s. The last, fitted with triple carburetors, could propel the car to 60 mph in 6.6 seconds. Fuel consumption was terrifying. The Panther Westwinds company belonged to Robert Jankel, who had worked for a car conversion company and then in the fashion industry. This unusual career trajectory may go some way toward explaining the ethos behind his products. The J72 didn't really look anything like an SS Jaguar – it was less elegant – but it was beautifully and solidly made. The interior trim was of especially high standard, employing walnut veneers and top-grade Connolly hide. A manual gearbox was fitted, lifted from the XJ6. Panther's other efforts included a couple of smaller, thirties-style roadsters: the Vauxhall-based Lima and the Ford-powered Kallista. The "luxury" Rio was built on a Triumph Dolomite platform. There was a super-sports coupé called the Solo and a nameless, six-wheeled prototype. Panther's masterpiece was the Jaguar V12-based DeVille, whose radiator was adorned with a cluster of amethysts! They were built, appropriately, close to the old Brooklands circuit.

| | |
|---|---|
| **ENGINE:** | Front-mounted, V12 |
| **CAPACITY:** | 5343 cc |
| **OUTPUT:** | 250 bhp @ 6000 rpm |
| **TOP SPEED:** | 122 mph |
| **ACCELERATION:** | 0–60 in 6.6 seconds |

# PANTHER DeVILLE 1974

The Surrey-built Panther was very close in spirit to the Californian Excalibur. They were both pastiches of classic automobiles, equipped with stock motors and running gear and finished to a very high standard. Quite what the appeal of such cars can be is difficult to gauge. If you want a vintage car, why not buy one? The Morgan is probably the only such machine that's authentic as its thirties styling has never changed – at least until the Aero. The Panther DeVille was supposedly modeled on the Bugatti Royale, but looked more like a J Series Duesenberg, the ultimate icon of Roaring Twenties excess. This image obviously appealed to the late Oliver Reed, who was an enthusiastic owner – a newspaper printed a picture of Mr Reed, dressed in Al Capone style, beside his DeVille, beneath the headline "Big, extravagant and drinks like a fish (and that's just the car …)." The DeVille's interior refinements included a refrigerated cocktail cabinet, and it could manage about 10 mpg. The tubular-framed monster rode a 142-inch wheel base and used V12 Jaguar mechanicals. A convertible was brilliantly cast as Cruella DeVille's car in the live action remake of the movie *101 Dalmatians*.

| | | | |
|---|---|---|---|
| **ENGINE:** | Front-mounted, V12 | **TOP SPEED:** | 130 mph |
| **CAPACITY:** | 5343 cc | **ACCELERATION:** | 0–60 in 7.0 seconds |
| **OUTPUT:** | 285 bhp @ 5500 rpm | | |

# PEGASO Z102 1955

The Pegaso, named after Perseus' winged steed, was built in Barcelona at the Calle
de Segrera works previously occupied by Hispano-Suiza. The Z102 was a car built
along similar lines in the sense that cost was not a consideration. With the exception
of the Bosch electrics, every component for these beautiful machines was produced
in-house. Coachwork was by either Touring of Milan or the exclusive Paris firm of
Russian-born Jacques Saoutchic. The Pegaso was a unitary design and was powered
by a light alloy 2.5-liter V8 with twin-cams per bank. These were at first chain-
driven, but later gears were installed. Up to four Weber carburetors were employed
and drive was transmitted via a five-speed gearbox mounted in the back axle.
Subsequent models were overbored, supercharged and generally tweaked to
produce additional horsepower. The Pegaso was fearsomely complex but exquisitely
engineered; its performance was excellent but it was just too expensive. The
company turned to making trucks, which it continues to do.

| | | | |
|---|---|---|---|
| **ENGINE:** | Front-mounted, V8 | **TOP SPEED:** | 125 mph |
| **CAPACITY:** | 2474 cc | **ACCELERATION:** | 0–60 in 10.3 seconds |
| **OUTPUT:** | 165 bhp @ 6500 rpm | | |

# PLYMOUTH ROAD RUNNER SUPERBIRD 1970

The Road Runner Superbird was just
about the ultimate example of the
American "muscle car." The Road
Runner – named for the popular,
animated avian that was pursued,
relentlessly but fruitlessly, by Wyle E.
Coyote – was based on the Plymouth
Belvedere and fitted, initially with
383 cid (6.5-liter) V8 tuned to deliver
325 bhp. The car was also fitted with
a horn that mimicked the cartoon
Road Runner's signature "Beep-beep!"
The Superbird was equipped with
"aerodynamic aids" that comprised a
massive fiberglass nosecone and a
towering rear spoiler – whose
primary function seems to have been
to carry the obligatory Road Runner
decal. The whole thing looked
preposterous but was capable of
phenomenal acceleration and straight-
line speed, particularly when
equipped with the optional 426 cid
(7-liter) block which developed
425 bhp. Street models, fitted with
the 440 cid Super Commando V8,
were capable of about 140 mph but
racing versions could hit 190mph!

| | |
|---|---|
| **ENGINE:** | Front-mounted, V8 |
| **CAPACITY:** | 440 cu. in. (7.2 liters) |
| **OUTPUT:** | 375 bhp @ 4600 rpm |
| **TOP SPEED:** | 140 mph |
| **ACCELERATION:** | 0–60 in 4.9 seconds |

# PONTIAC GTO 1964

The GTO was the first true "muscle car." It was basically a mid-size Pontiac Tempest with a 389 cid (6.5-liter) V8 tucked under the hood. A great legend has been created about the genesis and development of the GTO and Jim Wangers' book *Glory Days* details it in wonderful, evocative detail – from the clandestine supply of parts to a Detroit dealership, in a suburb called Windsor and named Royal Pontiac, through the development of the "Royal Bobcats," to the Saturday night "rumbles" on Woodward Avenue. Development was overseen by none other than John DeLorean. The GTO was one of Pontiac's Wide-Track models – so called because they had a wide track. The GTO took its name, most impertinently, from the magnificent Gran Turismo Omologato Ferrari sports-racer – *Road and Track* magazine played the two GTOs off against each other, pronouncing honors just about even. The classic GTO was a smart car, with its stacked headlights and uncluttered lines. A manual shift was common and one splendid optional extra was the hood-mounted tachometer. How could anyone resist that?

| ENGINE: | Front-mounted, V8 |
| --- | --- |
| CAPACITY: | 389 cu. in. (6.4 liters) |
| OUTPUT: | 325 bhp @ 4800 rpm |
| TOP SPEED: | 120 mph |
| ACCELERATION: | 0–60 in 6.9 seconds |

# PORSCHE 356 1950

Ferry Porsche, son of the legendary Ferdinand, creator of the Volkswagen, wanted to produce a sports car based on his father's plan. What was essentially a Beetle was clothed in wonderful bulbous "tin toy" bodywork and supplied with twin carburetors to bump the output up from 25 bhp to 40. The earliest examples were built in Austria, whence Dr Porsche had relocated during the Second World War. A cabriolet was offered as well as the coupé and, with production moved to more capacious premises in Stuttgart, engine size and state of tune were rapidly increased. By 1955, 1600 cc 356As could top 100 mph and the Carrera version could reach 125. The 356s were employed extensively in competition and many found their way to the United States, firmly establishing the marque's reputation there – despite the misfortune of Hollywood's heartthrob of the hour, James Dean, dying at the wheel of his Speedster. The final version, the 356C, remained in production until 1965.

| | |
|---|---|
| **ENGINE:** | Rear-mounted, Flat 4 |
| **CAPACITY:** | 1582 cc |
| **OUTPUT:** | 70 bhp @ 4500 rpm |
| **TOP SPEED:** | 101 mph |
| **ACCELERATION:** | 0–60 in 15.4 seconds |

# PORSCHE 911 1963

The Porsche 911 is a truly iconic sports car and has fanatical supporters throughout the world. The first model was introduced at the Frankfurt Motor Show in 1963. Though its VW ancestry was still plain to see, the 911 was a sleek shark of a car in contrast to the 356's globular guppy; the 911 represented refinement rather than mere novelty. At its heart, or rather in its hindquarters, was an air-cooled horizontally opposed six-cylinder engine and it had torsion-bar suspension. It sounds like a revised 356, but it was a revolutionary car. Its quickness and speed, right from the start, were hugely impressive, but unlike many high-performance cars, the 911 wasn't prone to oiling up or overheating in traffic – even in California, where it quickly established itself as an object of aspiration. Handling on early cars could be treacherous – entering a bend on a trailing throttle could spell disaster, but this was quickly overcome. Numerous versions continue to follow: the 911S, the 911T, with its distinctive "Targa" top. Fuel injection came with the 911S; a unique clutchless manual transmission – the Sportomatic – appeared, and so it continues, via Carreras and RSs and Turbos, to the present day.

| | |
|---|---|
| **Engine:** | Rear-mounted, Flat 6 cylinder |
| **Capacity:** | 1991 cc |
| **Output:** | 130 bhp @ 6100 rpm |
| **Top Speed:** | 130 mph |
| **Acceleration:** | 0–60 in 8.9 seconds |

# PORSCHE 928 1977

The 928 would have been the finest car ever produced by Porsche if only it had been a 911. In a radical departure from established practice, Porsche unveiled a front-engined V8-powered Grand Tourer at the Geneva Motor Show in 1977. It was greeted with disbelief. Contemporary reviewers compared the car to the Porsche 911, rather than to, say, the Jaguar XJS or the Mercedes coupés. Nobody seemed interested in the trans-axle gearbox or the handsome and distinctive styling, courtesy of Anatole Lapine. Most of all, nobody seemed to note how lovely it was to drive. Equally at home on an expressway or a winding lane, the 928 could be as exhilarating as most 911s but more relaxing than any. The public – most importantly, Porsche's public – just didn't get it. Performance increased until, in 1989, it became Porsche's fastest road car with a top speed of 170 mph and 330 bhp on tap. The Series 4 was followed by the GTS, both fabulous cars, but still the market failed to respond. The 928 was discontinued in 1995 and the world lost a great unrecognized classic car.

| | |
|---|---|
| **ENGINE:** | Front-mounted, V8 |
| **CAPACITY:** | 4474 cc |
| **OUTPUT:** | 240 bhp @ 5500 rpm |
| **TOP SPEED:** | 135 mph |
| **ACCELERATION:** | 0–60 in 8.0 seconds |

# PORSCHE 959 1983

The 959 is such stuff dreams as are made on ... the ultimate variation on the 911 theme. Introduced at the 1983 Frankfurt Motor Show, the 959 was required to achieve homologation for the company's latest Group B sports-racers. The familiar, seemingly indestructible, horizontally opposed six-cylinder engine was equipped with twin turbochargers and water-cooled cylinder heads. The four-wheel-drive system suffered from severe delays in development but arrived in early 1987, by which time a 959 had won the Paris–Dakar rally without it. Unlike many of its forebears, the 959 had no vices. The drive system was computer-controlled and ensured precisely the correct distribution of power to each wheel. A computer was also responsible for lowering ride height at high speeds – and with six-speed transmission, high speeds were easily attainable. Ride height could also be adjusted to cope with speed ramps and cart tracks: the car could be raised 7 inches if necessary. Porsche only needed to produce 200 959s, but in fact 250 were built, the last in 1988.

| | | | |
|---|---|---|---|
| **Engine:** | Rear-mounted, flat 6 | **Top Speed:** | 197 mph |
| **Capacity:** | 2849 cc | **Acceleration:** | 0–60 in 3.6 seconds |
| **Output:** | 450 bhp @ 6500 rpm | | |

# PORSCHE TURBO 1974

The Porsche 911 was a very good car with a very bad image. It reached its peak in the late seventies with the introduction of the 3.3 liter version, which became the ultimate object of Yuppie desire. With its flared arches and its "whale tail" spoiler, color-coded bodywork (usually Guards' red or black) and fat cat tires, it captured the zeitgeist of the eighties perfectly. It was a wad on wheels. It was also a magnificent machine, with a proud heritage that stretched back to the original 911 of 1962. The first turbocharged 911 debuted at the Paris Motor Show in 1974 and was marketed, in part, to homologate Porsche's 935 Group 4 racer. The 3-liter air-cooled flat-six was "blown" by a KKK unit to give 60 bhp more than its conventionally aspirated cousin, the Carrera. Acceleration was electrifying; it was the quickest car of its generation. Handling, unlike some early 911s, was excellent. The interior was beautifully appointed whilst retaining the functional simplicity that was Porsche's trademark. Best of all it was immensely tractable. It could shunt around the City all week and then sprint down to the country for the weekend without skipping a beat.

| **ENGINE:** | Rear-mounted, flat 6 | **TOP SPEED:** | 155 mph |
| **CAPACITY:** | 2993 cc | **ACCELERATION:** | 0–60 in 6.4 seconds |
| **OUTPUT:** | 260 bhp @ 5500 rpm | | |

# RENAULT ALPINE 1970

The Dieppe-built Alpine A110, successor to the much admired A106 and A108, was unveiled by Jean Redele at the Paris Motor Show in 1963. The styling of the fiberglass body was extremely modern and effective and the car was an instant hit. Over 15 years, fewer than 8000 examples were produced, making this a truly exclusive machine; surviving examples are as desirable to collectors as they were when they were new. The A110 was upgraded throughout its production run and enjoyed enormous success in Group Four rallying, winning three world championships in the late sixties and early seventies. Its reign only came to an end with the arrival of the all-conquering Lancia Stratos. Standard Renault motors were gas-flowed and fitted with twin Weber carburetors, larger inlets and stronger valve springs, plus special brake kits for mountain use. Despite its engine location, the Alpine's handling was excellent. It could be drifted through bends like a front-engined car but had the traction of a rear-engined car.

| | |
|---|---|
| **ENGINE:** | Rear-mounted, four cylinder. |
| **CAPACITY:** | 1565 cc |
| **OUTPUT:** | 138 bhp @ 6000 rpm |
| **TOP SPEED:** | 130 mph |
| **ACCELERATION:** | 0–60 in 7.0 seconds |

# RENAULT ALPINE GTA 1985

The Dieppe-based Alpine company had been closely associated with Renault for many years– with its earlier models using many Renault parts – and in 1975 Renault bought the company to prevent it going into receivership. The Renault Alpine GTA was the first new car launched afterwards, as a replacement for the Alpine A310. The GTA was far more elegant than its predecessor, with an angular shape, body-integrated bumpers, unique triangular C-pillars and a large rear windshield. It was also technically far more advanced, with the PRV V6 engine in a rear-engined layout and fiberglass body panels – making it considerably lighter and quicker than the rival steel-bodied Porsche 944. Famously roomy – it could carry four adults in comfort – the GTA was also a delight to drive, offering a smooth ride, easy cornering and precise gear changes. Unfortunately, it never really caught on and sales were poor. It was extensively updated as the A610 in 1991, but manufacturing ceased in 1995.

| | |
|---|---|
| **ENGINE:** | Rear-mounted, V6 |
| **CAPACITY:** | 2458 cc |
| **OUTPUT:** | 197 bhp @ 5750 rpm |
| **TOP SPEED:** | 155 mph |
| **ACCELERATION:** | 0–60 in 6.9 seconds |

# ROLLS-ROYCE CAMARGUE 1975

The Pininfarina-styled Camargue was, like the Corniche convertible, based on the Silver Shadow platform. It was hailed in the company's advertising as "The most beautiful Rolls-Royce ever built" but the public begged to differ. However, it was, except for the monstrous Phantom VI, the most expensive standard-bodied Rolls-Royce ever built and it may be this that appealed to buyers in the Middle East, where most Camargues seemed to end up. The coupé styling, with its large glass areas, forward-leaning radiator and twin headlights, was reminiscent of the car used by Lady Penelope in the successful animated puppet series *Thunderbirds*, though whether this influenced Rolls-Royce has not – like the car's horsepower and acceleration – been revealed officially. One innovation was the automatic split-level air-conditioning system, which allowed the occupants to decide whether they wanted hot heads and cold feet or vice versa. It was also the first Rolls-Royce to be designed using the metric system. Despite the Camargue's quite sporting demeanor – and performance, for such a large car, was very lively – a Bentley version was never offered, though one car was so badged to special order.

| | |
|---|---|
| **ENGINE:** | Front-mounted, V8 |
| **CAPACITY:** | 6750 cc |
| **OUTPUT:** | 285 bhp @ 5750 rpm |
| **TOP SPEED:** | 125 mph |
| **ACCELERATION:** | 0–60 in 10.5 seconds |

# STUDEBAKER AVANTI 1962

In 1852 the Studebaker brothers, Henry and Clement, had started out with a blacksmith's shop on the corner of Michigan Street and Jefferson Street in South Bend, Indiana. By 1868, their company was the largest wagon builder in the world. In 1902, Thomas Edison bought one of their electric cars, and they started making gasoline engines in 1904. Despite producing some excellent cars the company declined, and in the late 1950s Sherwood Ebert was taken on to try to turn around Studebaker's fortunes. Ebert turned to Raymond Loewy, who had been responsible for many Studebaker designs, and within two weeks, working in a rented house in Palm Springs, Florida, Loewy and his team had produced an eighth-scale clay model that was shipped to South Bend for appraisal. The Avanti looked like no other American car of the period – in fact, it looked like no other car. Loewy's styling was strangely transatlantic and the car's handling and performance were positively European – as was its name, of course. All this was too much for the purchasing public. Production ceased in South Bend in December 1963 and was shifted to Canada, where it lurched on for a further two years.

| | |
|---|---|
| **ENGINE:** | Front-mounted, V8 |
| **CAPACITY:** | 4725 cc |
| **OUTPUT:** | 210 bhp @ 4500 rpm |
| **TOP SPEED:** | 125 mph |
| **ACCELERATION:** | 0–60 in 8.2 seconds |

# SUNBEAM TIGER 1964

The Sunbeam Tiger was a stablemate of the AC Cobra, the legendary Carroll Shelby
having been closely involved in the design and development of both cars. As with
the Cobra, the Tiger had a powerful Ford V8 in a car that had originally been
intended for a far more modest power plant. The 7-liter Cobra had started out as
the 2-liter Ace; the 4.7-liter Tiger had once been the 1500 cc Alpine. Whereas the
AC was a British car manufactured largely in America, the Tiger was essentially an
American car, built in Britain. It was named, neatly, after Henry Segrave's 1926 land
speed record car, a V12 Sunbeam – Segrave himself had been half American. Jensen
Motors, which had considerable experience with American V8s, was given the task
of developing the prototype and an example was shown at the New York Motor
Show in 1964. Though they lacked the raw performance of the Cobras, Tigers were
quick cars for their day and scored a number of notable rally victories.

| | | | |
|---|---|---|---|
| **ENGINE:** | Front-mounted, V8 | **TOP SPEED:** | 120 mph |
| **CAPACITY:** | 4261 cc | **ACCELERATION:** | 0–60 in 9.4 seconds |
| **OUTPUT:** | 141 bhp @ 4400 rpm | | |

# TATRA 603 1958

The Tatra was built by a commercial vehicle company in Czechoslovakia. Hand-built in very small numbers, the 603 was developed from the T77 of 1934 and stayed in production until 1975 – and even then its design was unique and radical. The car was powered by a rear-mounted air-cooled V8 engine. The bulbous aerodynamic styling gave the car a peculiarly menacing look, an image that was doubtless enhanced by its association with senior Communist Party officials, for whom travel by Tatra was exclusively reserved. The interior was immensely spacious, giving decadent, Western-style limousine comfort. Handling was far better than might be imagined from its highly unorthodox mechanical layout, which bears a startling resemblance to Preston Tucker's "revolutionary" design of 1948. The 603 actually competed in a number of rallies and endurance events, being ideally suited to poor road conditions. The model was eventually replaced by the 613, which featured a quad-cam V8 and was styled by Vignale. The Tatra remains a unique and tantalizing vision of a Soviet future that might have been.

| | | | |
|---|---|---|---|
| **ENGINE:** | Rear-mounted, V8 | **TOP SPEED:** | 100 mph |
| **CAPACITY:** | 2472cc | **ACCELERATION:** | Not Available |
| **OUTPUT:** | 95 bhp @ 3000 rpm | | |

# TRIUMPH TR2 1952

A classic, British sports car, the TR2 was the first model in the long and much loved TR line. The car shown at the 1952 Earls Court Motor Show was designated the TR1 but by the time it reached the showroom it had advanced already. Powered by a solid Standard-Vanguard twin-carburetor, 2-liter engine, the TR was positively rakish, with a flowing wing line and cut-away doors; wire wheels were an optional extra and aero screens could be fitted to give a really sporting look. Performance was lively by the standards of the early fifties and about 8500 TR2s were produced, the vast majority being exported to the United States where they started the American love affair with the Triumph. The line continued through to the TR4A, which also incorporated independent rear suspension. TR5s were fitted with a six-cylinder engine, as was the TR6. The TR7 (and 8) are best not spoken of. The quality of the design and construction of the TR2 is borne out by the number that are still giving immense pleasure to drivers across the world. A classic, British sports car.

| | |
|---|---|
| **ENGINE:** | Front-mounted, four cylinder |
| **CAPACITY:** | 1991 cc |
| **OUTPUT:** | 90 bhp @ 4800 rpm |
| **TOP SPEED:** | 105 mph |
| **ACCELERATION:** | 0–60 in 12.0 seconds |

# TRIUMPH TR6 1969

The TR6 was the last of the "real" TRs and a worthy successor to a noble line. Over 90,000 were sold, making the "6" the most popular of all TRs, and with its smart modern Karmann styling and great practicality, it has become a highly usable and enjoyable modern classic. It was powered by a lusty six-cylinder engine, carried over from the TR5, which gave very strong performance – although the Bosch fuel-injection system could prove troublesome. Handling was above average for this style of British sports car as the independent rear suspension reduced the liability of "axle tramp" that was a feature of many of its contemporaries – the Alfa Spider and the Jensen Healey being two notable examples. Solid build quality also reduced the "scuttle shake" that bedeviled many similar convertibles – in fact, with the smart hardtop fitted, the TR6 was a very passable GT. Most, as ever, were exported to America. An overdrive transmission system was fitted that operated in third and fourth gears, giving improved fuel economy. Many TR6s were (and are) used in competition and a wide variety of performance parts have been produced for them.

| | |
|---|---|
| **Engine:** | Front-mounted, six cylinder |
| **Capacity:** | 2498 cc |
| **Output:** | 150 bhp @ 5500 rpm |
| **Top Speed:** | 125 mph |
| **Acceleration:** | 0–60 in 7.7 seconds |

# TUCKER 48 1948

Preston Tucker was, undoubtedly, a dreamer. In his youth, he had hung around at early motor sport events and, like so many boys, had become thoroughly hooked on the smell and the sound and the speed of the embryonic automobile. He wanted to create the ultimate car – the car of the future. The Tucker 48 was designed in Michigan and built in Chicago; the fastback styling was by Alex S. Tremulis and incorporated a three-headlight front, the central light being intended to "steer" with the front wheels. In June 1948, Tucker wrote "An open letter to the automobile industry in the interests of the American motorist." In it, he accuses the Dons of Detroit of attempting to sabotage his project, via corruption and subterfuge that extended even unto the US government. It's strangely infantile stuff; did Tucker really believe that the American public would prove any less conservative than the American auto industry when confronted with the idea of a car driven by a rear-mounted horizontally opposed six-cylinder engine? Would they not have preferred to stick with a big V8, mounted up-front? Strangest of all, his "revolutionary" design bears a striking resemblance to the 1934 Tatra T77 – a Communist car!

| | |
|---|---|
| **ENGINE:** | Rear-mounted, flat 6 |
| **CAPACITY:** | 335 cu. in. |
| **OUTPUT:** | 166 bhp |
| **TOP SPEED:** | 120 mph |
| **ACCELERATION:** | 0–60 in 10.0 seconds |

# TVR CERBERA 1994

The Blackpool-based TVR company was founded in 1958 by TreVoR Wilkinson. The Cerbera is named for Cerberus, the monstrous watchdog that guarded the entrance to Hades according to Greek myth; he had three heads and a mane of serpents. TVR's version is pretty scary too, but not so off-putting. First shown at the London Motor Show, it was the first hardtop TVR since the Tasmin and has 2+2 accommodation. The engines offered were two V8s and a straight 6, but even in its slowest form it was an exceptionally fast car. The dramatic styling was the work of an in-house TVR team who deliberately eschewed computer aided design in the early stages, relying on sketches and sculpted models. The result was an incredibly stylish and purposeful car. The design of the 75-degree V8 is competition-inspired and provides immense power while being lightweight and seemingly indestructible. Many TVRs are raced regularly and return, season after season, to the track, a testament to the quality of their design and construction.

| | | | |
|---|---|---|---|
| **ENGINE:** | Front-mounted, V8 | **TOP SPEED:** | 185 mph |
| **CAPACITY:** | 4185 cc | **ACCELERATION:** | 0–60 in 4.0 seconds |
| **OUTPUT:** | 350 bhp @ 6500 rpm | | |

# TVR GRIFFITH 1990

TVR's production totals about 1500 cars a year. Like all of them, the Griffith was hand-built, and finished to a very high standard. Clothed in traditionally-styled fiberglass bodywork, the Griffith had a race-bred lightweight chassis that was well able to handle the massive output of its 5-liter V8 engine, which provided astonishing acceleration as well as a very high top speed. The first "Griffith" debuted in 1963. An American Ford 289 (4.7 liter) V8 had somehow been shoehorned into the Grantor's body and chassis and drove through the original BMC rear axle. Surprisingly, perhaps, the car drove and handled well. The new Griffith represents a great improvement on the original, and on the company's wedge-shaped offerings of the 1980s, not only in terms of performance but also in all-around build quality. In a decade, TVR has gone from being a glorified kit-car to a machine that can stand comparison to the most exclusive exotics. Power-assisted steering was a welcome addition, as the Griffith was otherwise almost unparkable.

| | | | |
|---|---|---|---|
| **ENGINE:** | Front-mounted, V8 | **TOP SPEED:** | 155 mph |
| **CAPACITY:** | 4988 cc | **ACCELERATION:** | 0–60 in 4.1 seconds |
| **OUTPUT:** | 325 bhp @ 5500 rpm | | |

# TVR SAGARIS 2006

The styling of the TVR Sagaris –
though still extremely aggressive – is
far more effective than the ungainly
six-eyed version of the Tuscan, which
looked very much as though it had
been designed and built in
somebody's garden shed. And its
performance is nothing short of
incredible. Developed from the T350,
a huge amount of work has been done
on maximizing the new car's
downforce in order to improve
stability. The track is wider than the
350's and power is supplied by
TVR's straight-six engine, tuned to
develop close to 400 bhp. This is a
genuinely lightweight car, and gives
phenomenal acceleration and an
astronomic top speed. The extensive
employment of cooling vents in the
composite bodywork points to
competition intent and the Sagaris
must surely be a Le Mans contender.
TVR carries out extensive testing on
all its models in a wide variety of
locations and conditions, aiming to
ensure a reliability that matches their
tremendous performance.

| | |
|---|---|
| **ENGINE:** | Front-mounted, six cylinder |
| **CAPACITY:** | 3996 cc |
| **OUTPUT:** | 400 bhp @ 7000 rpm |
| **TOP SPEED:** | 195 mph |
| **ACCELERATION:** | 0–60 in 3.7 seconds |

# VAUXHALL VX220 2002

The VX220 and the new VXR220 Turbo, from GM's Opel/Vauxhall subsidiary, offer uncompromising handling and performance for the price of a family sedan. With its Astra-based motor, the VX gives not only blistering acceleration and a seriously illegal top speed but also powerful and progressive mid-range acceleration for swift and safe overtaking. It provides a competition car experience while remaining (pretty much) practical transport. Early models, following Lotus's example, were extremely spartan, but customer feedback has led to more interior refinement. It is obvious that these cars are being used for everyday motoring rather than as "something for the weekend." Having said that, if two people want to go away for the weekend in one, there is sufficient luggage space; if it rains, the hood is waterproof; if the sun shines, the top stows easily. Driving is fun: gear shifting, via the Vauxhall Vectra's five-speed cable-operated transmission, is slick and feels direct; ABS brakes are fitted and the car's handling is razor-sharp. Perhaps the car's only drawback is its Vauxhall badge. If the VX220 were a Lotus, it'd be a great Lotus.

| | |
|---|---|
| **Engine:** | Mid-mounted, four cylinder |
| **Capacity:** | 1998 cc |
| **Output:** | 200 bhp @ 5500 rpm |
| **Top Speed:** | 151 mph |
| **Acceleration:** | 0–60 in 4.7 seconds |

# VOLVO P1800S 1960

Jaguar passed up the request to supply an E-Type as The Saint's *Hirondel* and so, for the seminal sixties television show, Roger Moore ended up behind the wheel of a new Volvo, giving welcome exposure and a considerable image boost. The P1800 was a stylish departure from Volvo's established image as the constructor of safe, solid, staid Swedish cars. It was a very reasonably priced, elegantly styled, beautifully detailed, two-seater touring coupé. A Frua-built prototype was shown in Brussels, in January 1960, but under an unusual agreement the P1800 was to be assembled by Jensen Motors in West Bromwich – even though up to that point Jensen's experience was with fiberglass-bodied cars. The arrangement was short-lived, as the steel body panels suffered corrosion damage en route to Jensen. Production was switched to Sweden after a mere 6000 cars had been completed and the model designation changed to P1800S to reflect this.

| | |
|---|---|
| **ENGINE:** | Front-mounted, four cylinder |
| **CAPACITY:** | 1778 cc |
| **OUTPUT:** | 100 bhp @ 5800 rpm |
| **TOP SPEED:** | 105 mph |
| **ACCELERATION:** | 0–60 in 13.4 seconds |

# CARS THROUGH THE DECADES

# 1940S – RECONSTRUCTION

During the Second World War much of the production capacity in automobile factories had been turned over to the manufacture of military vehicles, and the shortage of fuel in many countries meant that there were few buyers for new cars. So, in both the United States and Europe, most cars offered in the immediate post-war years were simply variations on pre-war models. However, one thing that had moved on in massive leaps and bounds as a result of the war was technology – and the huge advances that had been made soon began to affect every new automobile. For the moment engineering drove the show, and styling was forced to take a back seat. Many cars of the forties were big, solid and dependable-looking – reflecting a need for a sense of stability after all the upheaval of wartime. Cars became more rounded, sleek and streamlined – but not for aesthetic reasons; engineers were beginning to take on board the principles of aerodynamics from the aircraft industry.

*Below: The Jaguar XK120*
*Oposite: The Ford Thunderbird*

## 1950S – FINS AND CHROME

After the bleakness of the 40s – dark, depressing and austere – the world stood on the brink of a brighter future at the beginning of the 1950s. American servicemen stationed in Europe had fallen in love with cars that were cheap, fun and simple to maintain – such as the MG TA Midget – and it didn't take American manufacturers long to develop their own versions, such as the Corvette and the Thunderbird. An increase in disposable income meant cars were available to a larger market – but the new middle classes weren't seeking restrained luxury, they wanted flashy cars to prove they had arrived. This was the beginning of America's love affair with the automobile, when it ceased to be practical transport and became an object of desire, a style statement and a status symbol. For the first time the stylists could overrule the engineers, who were forced to take some of their wilder ideas and actually make a car that would run. Chrome abounded, "Dagmars" appeared on bumpers and throughout the decade the rear wings sprouted ever-bigger fins. Legendary stylist Harley Earl also came up with the world's first wrap-around windshield – on the Cadillac Eldorado.

# 1960S – SWINGING SIXTIES

Whatever else they may be perceived as, the 60s were a reaction – or rather a revolution. Discipline, order and respect had served their purpose and had their day and the times they were a-changin' – forever. Young people not only rebelled against their parents' values – they also rebelled against waste and extravagance, particularly in their choice of car. These new consumers weren't seeking flashy status symbols – they wanted small, cheap, unpretentious cars, but they also wanted decent performance. This was the era of the Mini Cooper, a tiny car that had room for four people; it was nippy, it was safe, it was cheap and – due to its novelty – classless. It rapidly became a symbol of Swinging London. In America the motor industry was suffering after the downturn in the economy at the end of the 50s, so manufacturers were looking for a way of producing new models that weren't too new, because that would be too expensive. The big success of this period was the Ford Mustang, which established a new class of performance automobile called the "pony car." The Mustang was produced almost entirely out of stock parts and was based on the existing compact platform of another Ford model.

*Below: The Mini Cooper S*
*Opposite above: The Ford Mustang*
*Opposite below: The Lotus Elan*

# 1970S – SEVENTIES CHIC

The seventies, to many, is the decade that time forgot. Sandwiched between the anarchy of the sixties and the avarice of the eighties, the period conjures images of Vietnam, the rise of terrorism and some of the grimmest fashions in recorded history. The automobile industry was hit by a double blow: the OPEC oil embargo – which suddenly proved that gasoline was not going to be plentiful and cheap forever – and new government regulations on emissions, fuel economy and safety. All of which had to be accommodated by the automobile designers under severe funding restraints. Stylists were pushed to the background again, the engineers took over and cars became more elegant and subdued. Power was increasing and performance became the new buzzword; the first turbocharged road car – the BMW 2002 Turbo – was introduced in 1972. Two of the defining features that changed the look of seventies cars were the introduction of the spoiler – which was added to improve stability at high speeds – and the widespread use of "Go-Faster" stripes – which added nothing to the actual performance of the car, but looked good to all those Boy Racers.

*Above: The Lamborghini Countach, complete with spoiler*

*Below: The Porsche Turbo*

# 1980S – THE YUPPIE YEARS

The 80s were the Yuppie Years. Deregulated and derestricted, the market decided that there was loads of money, more than enough for any number of fast cars. Speed was king and the engineers were happy to oblige. At the same time, many buyers of top-range cars were grown-up children of the sixties and they had their environmental credentials to think of. They wanted powerful, fast, expensive cars – but they also demanded hi-tech functionalism rather than self-indulgent fripperies. Macho culture required cars that were brutal to look at – often with spartan interior comforts – but packed raw performance and were beautiful to drive. A new golden age of sports car racing began, one that many regard as the greatest in history. The prestige of marques such as Ferrari, Porsche, Lotus, Maserati, Alfa Romeo, Mercedes Benz, Jaguar and Aston Martin came in part from their success in sports car racing and the road cars developed by these manufacturers were in many cases very similar in both styling and engineering to their race cars. Automobile engineers also began to employ lightweight materials – such as Kevlar and carbon fiber, which had been developed for F1 racing – in road cars to cut weight and maximize performance.

*Above: The Audi Quattro Sport*
*Below: The Ferrari Testarossa*

# 1990S – THE NAUGHTY NINETIES

Most countries across the developed world experienced the 90s as a prosperous time. Political stability and the spread of democracy led to a general feeling that "all was right with the world." Personal wealth was apparently growing and a higher standard of living became available for many. It was also a period of rapid growth in the field of technology when inventions which were previously cutting edge moved into the mainstream – personal computers became the norm, and the Internet was no longer just a novelty for the few. The automobile industry began to diversify and introduced the "multi-purpose" vehicle, in which performance was married to styling that in previous decades would have been deemed more suitable for a family car. It was in response to market demand – those who drove 4x4s or vans no reason why they should forgo the kind of power available to sports car drivers. Performance motors were no longer only made by a few manufacturers – everyone wanted to get in on the act, including new companies from the East. Ferocious performance was available in some models – the Corvette ZR1 even had a valet key in case an unwary driver unleashed the power of the engine unwittingly.

# 2000S – THE NEW MILLENNIUM

The dawning of a new age encourages introspection – people look back on what has gone before and wonder what lies ahead. The motor industry had been suffering a malaise, and many newer models have looked to earlier glory years for their inspiration, to an age when life was simpler. Retro styling has became popular – as in the Aston Martin Vanquish and the Corvette C6 Z06 – and new cars sometimes bore famous names from the past – such as the Bugatti Veyron. Despite the retro look, impressive performance and levels of safety now come as standard, coupled with state-of-the-art technology and materials. Passenger comfort is also very important – but at a price; cars are often offered with long lists of luxury options. Customizing has always been popular in some segments of the market, but is now big business – each purchaser of a Ferrari Enzo is invited to the factory to have the car individually tailored to their personal measurements and specific requirements.

*Opposite: The Corvette ZR1*
*Below: The Aston Martin Vanquish*

# INDEX

To
John Hodges

Acknowledgments

Thank you to my wife, Fleur, for her help and support while I was writing this book, to Marie Clayton for being a great editor, to Tim Wright and Kathy Ager at LAT for their excellent picture research and Alastair Staley for his help in scanning the images. Special thanks to Philip Jan "Enzo" van Sandwyk for all his help with research.

All images courtesy of LAT except those on pages 61, 76–7, 94–5, 203 and 206–7 which are courtesy of The National Motor Museum/MPL.